Mediterranean Weather Handbook for Sailors

Roberto Ritossa

Imray Laurie Norie & Wilson Ltd

Published by
Imray Laurie Norie and Wilson Ltd
Wych House The Broadway St Ives Cambridgeshire PE27 5BT England
☎ +(0)1480 462114 Fax +(0)1480 496109
www.imray.com
2008

1st edition 2008

British Library Cataloguing in Publication Data. A catalogue record for this book is available from the British Library.

ISBN 978 184623 068 4

CAUTION

While every care has been taken to ensure accuracy, neither the Publishers nor the Author will hold themselves responsible for errors, omissions or alterations in this publication. They will at all times be grateful to receive information which tends to the improvement of the work.

PLANS

The plans in this guide are not to be used for navigation. They are designed to support the text and should at all times be used with navigational charts.

Printed in Singapore by Star Standard Industries

Contents

Preface

Roberto Ritossa first set foot on a boat aged six, on an old leaking wooden Star.

He has changed a few boats since, cruised the Mediterranean for more than a dozen thousand miles and participated in several offshore races (Middle Sea Race, Rimini–Corfu–Rimini, etc). Over the years he accumulated a wealth of notes, local tips, books and research about weather, which at some point he decided to put all together.

He is a yacht architect (though not by profession), a few of his designs are still sailing around the world. He is also a radioamateur (M0ITA) and journalist.

A few years ago he went against the major migratory flow and left the Mediterranean to enjoy sailing in northern European waters. His current boat is berthed in Brittany.

Introduction

'Light, variable winds with possible gales later, returning light and variable'

Mediterranean sailors would probably suggest this as the most appropriate bulletin for their area of predilection: wind behaviour appears unpredictable, and weather is often observed to change from benign to life threatening in a matter of minutes.

The Mediterranean Sea is indeed a very difficult area for analysis and forecasting, as the various elements contributing to determine the weather show a particularly complex interaction. Compared for example to forecasts prepared for the open ocean, there are several specific factors making the Mediterranean Sea a more complex forecasting area.

First, important differences in land thermal characteristics exist among the colder continental regions to the north, areas like northern Africa to the south, the Balkans or for example the Iberian peninsula, just to name a few.

These varying heat behaviours have a direct influence over the different air masses interacting over the sea: cold, continental polar air from the northern European regions; hot, dry air from the African desert; moist maritime flows from the Atlantic Ocean, etc.

Then as they move, air masses meet many orographic features along their path: relief abounds all around Mediterranean shores, or in the case of the Apennines they basically cut it in two, mountainous islands of varying dimensions are scattered over its surface, several gaps exist along these orographic systems (Gibraltar, the river valleys of southern France, the Gulf of Gabes, just to name a few), etc. As they travel through uneven terrain, the physical characteristics of the different types of air (like temperature, humidity content, pressure, wind speed, etc.) undergo continuous modifications, both at the level of large scale phenomena spread over a thousand miles, and at the level of local scale features influencing weather over a few dozen of miles only.

On top of that, if weather systems originated elsewhere intervene (like for example a depression and its associated frontal system approaching from the Atlantic Ocean), they will be in their turn modified by the peculiar thermal and orographic characteristics of the Mediterranean, sometimes losing their former identity, at other times mixing with existing features, or even originating new weather systems.

Land and air characteristics, orography, etc. all these factors increase the complexity of the mutual relationships of temperature, humidity, pressure, etc., eventually increasing the variety of observed weather.

In the middle of these seemingly chaotic, inordinate atmospheric flows sits the Mediterranean Sea itself: a wide basin of rather gentle temperature water, enclosed by differing land features all around, where smaller scale, more unpredictable elements have a greater importance over weather and make the area one of the most difficult for forecasting.

Several weather services have developed complex models to analyze and forecast Mediterranean weather evolution, yet if supercomputers are fed by increasingly accurate data and detailed models, forecasting Mediterranean weather is and remains a very difficult task.

The purpose of this book is to give a general understanding of the various phenomena concurring to determine weather in the Mediterranean, and provide useful forecasting aids.

It is written for sailors, not meteorologists; theory is kept to a minimum, while every effort is made to provide clear interpretative tools which will be helpful in understanding actual weather and in forecasting its likely future evolution.

The text takes the point of view of sailors whose forecasting tools are usually limited to radio bulletins, weather charts obtained at the marina office or by radiofax, maybe a few GRIB files, the ubiquitous barometer, etc.

As internet resources and in particular web browsing aboard are still confined to a very limited number of yachts of bigger size, specialized forecasting tools of little practical relevance to the average cruiser like satellite picture analysis have not been considered.

However, as internet has become the most important channel of weather information dissemination, a comprehensive list of interesting internet addresses is given at the end of the book, should gales force to a longer stay in port waiting for a suitable weather window before casting off, or just to keep up with weather evolution while at home.

Being aimed at sailors, wind characteristics – speed and direction – are examined more in depth than other weather elements like precipitation or cloudiness. There is a lot of truth in saying that if Mediterranean weather is good and pleasant most of the time, making it an excellent cruising area, strong winds can arise in a very short time and generate difficult situations, both for boats at sea and at anchor. Whether they are widespread or localised over a limited area, both can be equally dangerous and represent a hazard for sailing boats. For this reason, a particular attention is devoted to situations where wind force may rise upwards of 5/6 Beaufort (around 20–25 knots), which for the average size boat represent the boundary between fair weather sailing and increasingly tougher conditions.

General characteristics of lighter winds like sea breezes are discussed too, even if local peculiarities take their toll over the forecaster and often cause all sort of discrepancies which, if of higher importance to the racer, are much less so for the cruiser.

The structure of the book is as follows:

- First, an overview of Mediterranean climatology is given, with a description of the seasonal behaviour of the main weather elements: wind, pressure, temperatures, etc. We advise everyone to read this chapter before jumping to other sections of the book.

- Then as some strong wind developments are related to drifting low pressure areas and their characteristics usually reflect the typical wind pattern around depressions, while other winds are more related to Mediterranean peculiarities and are often given a particular name (mistral, meltemi, bora, etc), Chapter 2 and Chapter 3 describe the two broad categories.

- The main processes leading to generation (or strengthening) of depressions in the Mediterranean are described. From west to east, it will be shown how depressions develop over the Balearic islands, over north west Africa, in the Gulf of Genoa and in the Ionian, and how they affect the different sea areas.

- Next are considered the few regional wind systems which are spread over large bodies of water: Mistral, Sirocco, Tramontana, Gregale and Levante. These account for a great share of gales and storms in the whole Mediterranean.

- Both depressions and regional winds can be equally dangerous: the likely evolution of lows should be considered with as much care as the potential development of different pressure patterns leading to the strong regional winds which are described in the text.

- In Chapter 4, the whole Mediterranean basin is divided into eight sea areas: Strait of Gibraltar/Alboran, western Mediterranean, west central Mediterranean, Tyrrhenian Sea, Adriatic Sea, Ionian Sea, Aegean Sea, Eastern Mediterranean. The contribution of the low pressure systems and winds seen in the previous chapters, and the main characteristics of purely local phenomena (Vendaval, Meltemi, Bora, Cyprus depressions etc. just to name a few) are described for each of these areas. Appropriate references to the General sections are made when necessary.

- VHF channels for coastal weather forecasts are also indicated at the end of each *Sea Area section*. However, as forecasts for every area are usually available from a wide variety of sources, both national and foreign, and as each of these sources usually serves several sea areas, for practical reasons all the information about *How to get weather information* has been grouped in *Appendix I. Shortwave radio, Navtex, radiofax, RTTY*, etc. schedules and short descriptions are given for all the available services, together with a list of several relevant internet sites.

- *Appendix II* provides twelve monthly sets of wind roses located in offshore areas all over the Mediterranean, which with a bit of caution can be helpful in passage planning.

- In *Appendix III* cruisers will find a dictionary of the main meteorological terms used in foreign language bulletins.

- Sailors wanting to have an overview of weather features of the whole Mediterranean can read this book from the first page onward. If on the contrary there are plans to sail in a particular area, (say chartering in the Ionian, or delivering a boat from Cannes to Gibraltar), one can jump to the relevant geographic sections and get a more specific description of local weather features. Appropriate references to the General sections are made when necessary, in order to keep information as complete as possible.

The situations leading to the development of strong winds described in the book are those usually showing a higher degree of likelihood.

As a phenomenon is described (like a particular low pressure, or a strong regional wind), a series of symptoms or factors leading to its development is usually indicated: obviously, the higher the number of converging signs, and the higher their concordance with actual weather observations, the higher will the likelihood of that phenomenon be.

Obviously, it should not be forgotten that other different evolutions are possible, and wind or depressions behaviour always has a varying degree of uncertainty: important weather phenomena may well develop outside of the more likely, frequent patterns which are the objective of this work.

In other words, if no meteorology book can ever guarantee fair weather sailing, this text will hopefully provide the necessary tools to ascertain the likelihood of the greatest number of strong wind episodes.

In terms of passage planning, the rule that the best approach is to keep the highest degree of elasticity as to departure date or time is somewhat less effective in the Mediterranean.

It is of course true that being able to adapt one's departure date by a few days may mean the difference between a wet beat against a strong sirocco, an exhilarating run before a fresh gregale …or having to motor all the way because there is no wind.

Sometimes a night passage after having spent the daylight hours at anchor in a sheltered cove might be preferable where winds tend to abate at night, and so on.

On the other hand, cruisers should always keep in one tiny corner of their minds that ironic bulletin 'Light, variable winds with possible gales later, returning light and variable', as in terms of sudden changes in weather, the Mediterranean is second to none. Even during the best summer sailing days, it is always advisable to keep an open eye trying and catch the typical signs of possible worsening conditions: developing surface pressure and upper level chart patterns, sky and sea conditions, local barometric readings, 'further outlook' broadcast through bulletins, etc.

Any effort in that direction will likely reduce the probability of encountering bad weather, or at least will allow being better prepared: the more those indices converge, the more they should be considered with attention.

On a lighter note, if a lot of the attention goes towards stronger winds description and forecasting as they are the main concern for sailors, one should not forget that especially during the summer months moderate and breeze-like winds accompanied by fair weather will hopefully be the most common occurrence, and cruising will be a very pleasant experience.

Welcome to the Mediterranean!

1. Climatic and seasonal patterns overview

WINTER

Winters are generally mild. Extremely cold weather, although not unknown, is rare and usually does not last long. It is most confined to the northern areas, where often air masses are of cold continental origin.

Both the Iceland depression and the Açores high have drifted southward, with the latter often remaining below 40°N latitude. Eastern continental Europe is under the influence of the Siberian high, the most stable weather feature during this period of the year.

Over the whole Mediterranean, high pressure areas or ridges are routinely replaced by depressions (Gulf of Genoa, Ionian Sea, Aegean Sea, etc), which in turn drift to leave room for other high pressure areas, and so on giving the weather a marked variability.

The polar front activity routinely spreads into the western Mediterranean, and sometimes even weakened systems from the NW are quickly strengthened by the relatively warmer waters of the Mediterranean, generating heavy weather.

On average, northwesterly flows are common in the western/central Mediterranean, whereas southerly weather is statistically more frequent in the eastern/central basin.

Gale and storm force winds percentage is highest (about twice as much as during summer): areas like the Golfe du Lion, the Aegean Sea and the Adriatic Sea are among those where gales are more frequent and depressions usually form; the Gulf of Genoa is one of the most active cyclogenetic areas existing in the world, especially in winter but in summer too.

Mediterranean low pressure systems usually follow an easterly path throughout the area. Precipitation frequency is highest, especially in the northern regions of the area, together with fog formations.

Winds

On average, winds often blow from the W and NW quadrants, with an average force of 4Bft.

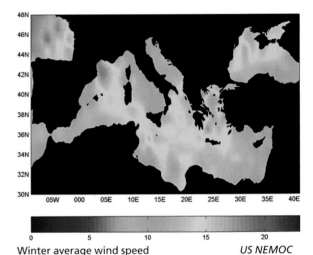

Winter average wind speed   *US NEMOC*

In the western and central Mediterranean prevailing winds are either westerly or easterly, in the Tyrrhenian Sea there is no predominant wind direction, the Adriatic often sees winds from the NE or SW quadrant, in the Aegean Sea the highest frequency winds are usually from the north (with southerlies a close second), in the eastern Mediterranean easterlies and northeasterlies predominate.

Sea breezes are a much less common occurrence than in summer; when they occur, they may not begin until noon.

Gales are a common occurrence during all the season. Areas where they are most likely include Golfe du Lion (an impressive 20% of the time near the coast, while 10% on the open sea), the Aegean Sea and the Adriatic Sea, both with frequencies of around 10%. Local phenomena can also determine increases in gale frequency: an example is the funnelling effect of Gibraltar Strait and adjacent Alboran Sea, where strong wind frequency is higher than in the surrounding areas.

Notwithstanding the high frequency of gales, calm days with sunny skies and mild temperatures are not unknown. Again, during winter, a marked variability seems to be the only constant.

Pressure

The difference in temperature between the sea and the adjacent land helps creating an area of low pressure over the water, surrounded by areas of relatively higher pressure over land. The warmer sea also contributes to reinforce frontal systems coming into the Mediterranean from the Atlantic Ocean.

Low pressure is generally found over Corse and Sardinia islands; whereas high pressure areas tend to develop as extensions of the Açores high over Spain or north western Africa, or extensions of the Asian high over eastern continental Europe.

Clouds and precipitation

Air flows meeting the warm waters of the sea (be it cold maritime polar air, or warmer southerly flows) become unstable and loaded with humidity, increasing cloud cover over the region.

Cloud cover maxima are located in the western Mediterranean area. Cloudy day averages are around 2/3 for the western area, 1/2 for the central Mediterranean and 1/4 for the eastern seas.

Cloudiness is usually more pronounced in the early morning, with stratus formations; after sunrise it usually decreases, to peak again in the afternoon.

During winter precipitation is at its highest, but it still is noticeable during the late autumn and early springtime. Geographically, it is concentrated in the northern areas, decreasing to a minimum in the northern shores of the African continent.

Rain is generally associated with the transit of depressions; it is highest in cold fronts, where warm moist air comes in contact with cold, dry air, and more important during the easterly transit of Atlantic depressions over the Iberian peninsula.

Thunderstorms are common in winter, especially in the eastern parts of the sea; they also occur when warm and moist sirocco winds are lifted by orographic features in the colder northern parts of the area.

Days of poor visibilities are common in the north. Thick fog usually develops when warm and moist sirocco transits over the relatively colder waters of the north, especially in the northern Adriatic, Gulf of Genoa, Golfe du Lion.

Radiation fog sometimes happens in the early morning of windless days, but usually it quickly disappears after sunrise.

Southern and eastern Mediterranean usually show clearer skies, fog is rare.

Temperature and humidity

Temperature is usually slightly higher in the southern parts of the Mediterranean, especially towards the east; whereas the lowest extremes are usually reached in January and February in the Golfe du Lion, north Adriatic Sea and north Aegean Sea (where snow, although rare, is not unknown).

Relative humidity is highest during winter, with maxima located in the western Mediterranean.

It usually increases during the night hours, and is heavily influenced by the prevailing wind regime. Sea breezes usually increase humidity, while offshore winds - especially those coming from African regions - usually make it drop.

The seasonal variation is highest in the northern area and very small along the north African coast.

SUMMER

During summer, the Açores high drifts northward, with a ridge over the Mediterranean which usually brings fair weather; sometimes though a weakening of the ridge allows low pressure systems and fronts to reach the western basin, but with less strength than during winter.

The eastern Mediterranean is under the strong influence of a wide field of relatively low pressure extending from Asia to northern Africa, which usually generates N–NE winds currents over the basin. These winds usually bring stability in the lower layers of the atmosphere, with fine and sunny weather.

Summers are usually hot, with fair weather. On average, strong winds are not too frequent, but by all means can and do happen in a few areas: mistral force winds in the central Mediterranean, meltemi winds in the Aegean Sea, etc. The sky is generally clear with good visibilities; fog is usually rare except in the early mornings.

Winds

Average wind speeds over the Mediterranean are 2–3Bft. The general description of wind directions given for the winter season remains basically the same, except for the Aegean Sea where winds from the southern quadrants become rare.

Land and sea breeze phenomena are common throughout all the area, and more frequent from early springtime to early autumn. On average, sea breeze usually starts at 0700 or 0800 local time, slowly increases until reaching a maximum of 4Bft in the early afternoon, wind speed then remains constant until 1800–1900, when the wind

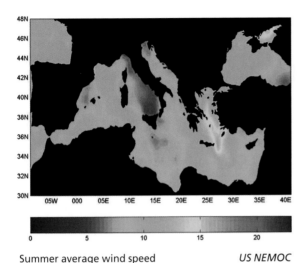

Summer average wind speed   *US NEMOC*

eventually dies away. Night time land breezes are somewhat weaker, averaging 3Bft. Sea and land breezes effects are usually felt up to 10–20M from the coast, and are heavily influenced by local orography.

Pressure

Pressure distribution remains fairly stable, with the Açores high extending over the northern area and an area of relatively low pressure over Asia minor. During the day, thermal lows may develop or intensify over land, and their effects are not much different from sea-land breezes. Moving storms are rare.

Clouds and precipitation

Mediterranean cloud cover is very low during the summer season, with most places showing an average of only one cloudy day out of ten.

Coastal cloudiness usually peaks in the afternoon, when cumulus development is at its maximum. Evenings and nights are usually clear.

Precipitation is generally associated with disturbances: examples are cold air coming from northern Europe over the sea, warm air flows coming out of northern Africa, or developing low pressure systems (the Genoa area shows a slightly higher percentage of rainy days). The south of the Mediterranean is very dry.

Temperature and humidity

Temperatures are usually higher in the southern and eastern regions of the Mediterranean Sea. Particularly hot days are frequent in areas adjacent to north African shores, especially when light sirocco winds bring hot Saharan air over the sea; they are also frequent where adiabatic heating is taking place, when air flows downwards from mountain chains, for example in Corsica and Sicily islands, or Greek mountains.

Relative humidity is low, with a minimum during the months of July and August. Seasonal variations are important in the northern area, and almost nil along the edge of the African coast.

The short term variation of relative humidity is often determined by winds: offshore breezes lower the level of moisture in the air, whereas sea breezes usually have higher humidity content.

Also, variations in temperature can cause variations in relative humidity: temperature decreases during the night can bring an increase in relative humidity even if the air water content itself has not changed much.

Thunderstorms Thunderstorms can be a very common weather event during the summer months. Their frequency decreases from north to south: the maximum is situated in the north Adriatic (with some places having as much as 6 or 7 days of thunderstorms per summer month), the minimum is along the coast of Libya and Egypt.

In other areas of the northern Mediterranean, thunderstorms can also form when moist sirocco winds are lifted by orographic features, like Pyrenees, Alps, Apennines, etc.

SPRING

In the Mediterranean, spring weather is usually characterized by a quick transition from summer type weather to winter type.

The area of high pressure over the Asian continent weakens, and a relatively low pressure area develops over Turkey. The Açores high ridge shifts slightly northward of its winter position and continues to influence the Mediterranean.

Throughout the area, developing low pressure areas circulating eastward are fewer than in winter; likewise, gale and storm winds frequency reduces to roughly 50% that of winter, becoming rarer and weaker as the season advances.

The average wind speeds drop to 9 to 13 knots. Sea breezes slightly increase in frequency.

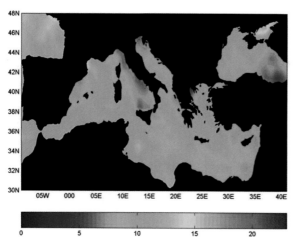

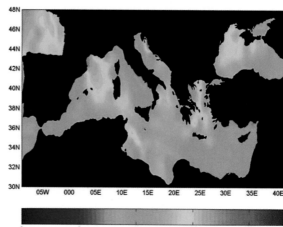

Spring average wind speed   *US NEMOC*

Autumn average wind speed   *US NEMOC*

Poor visibilities are still common especially in the northern and western Mediterranean, whereas in the south and east areas they are quickly decreasing in frequency, with most locations having less than three days per month with low visibility.

Low visibility in a belt of 30–50 miles along the north African coast is sometimes caused by dust storms: desert dust is brought along by hot southerly winds blowing from the African continent, especially in the area ahead of a cold front passage; usually they last less than one day, and most of the dust is cleared from the air by precipitation in the cold air area of the depression. Fog frequency is highest in the north Mediterranean where waters are cooler, especially when areas like the Gulf of Genoa, north Adriatic or Golfe du Lion are under the influence of southerly winds. Coastal fog can happen early in the morning on days with light, variable winds, but usually disappears at sunrise.

AUTUMN

Like spring, autumn is a transition season, often showing an abrupt change from summer type weather to a winter type one.

Wind speed increases a little, to an average 7–10 knots.

Land and sea breezes are still common, the first averaging 5–10 knots, while sea breezes are roughly one Beaufort notch higher, with an average 10–15 knots. Like in spring, the sea breeze onset is usually delayed until later in the morning.

The number of depressions begins to increase, as well as their strength; except for the low pressure area over Turkey, which weakens considerably.

Thunderstorms and heavy showers are still frequent, caused by the high residual heat of the sea waters. They can affect the whole of the Mediterranean, with a higher frequency in the central and southern Adriatic, Sicily strait, Athens area and north eastern Mediterranean.

2. Pressure features

Pressure distribution is generally the most important cause of strong wind development.

While high pressure areas may sometimes contribute to generate gale force winds (for example some types of Bora winds in the Adriatic Sea), depressions are the main factor behind most strong wind episodes occurring in the Mediterranean.

Whether they form over the sea (like the Gulf of Genoa or the Aegean Sea) or in adjacent areas (Atlantic Ocean, Sahara desert, etc), whether they transit over wide areas of the sea or remain confined on land beyond the shoreline, depressions may easily generate gale to strong gale force winds, sometimes reaching even storm or violent storm force.

Lows can develop anywhere in the Mediterranean. There are a few areas though where for a number of reasons depressions occur with a definitely higher frequency: as they have a significant impact on the weather of major parts of the Mediterranean, they will be the object of the following sections.

At other times instead weather charts may show several areas of relatively lower pressure, with no one really dominating the others. This is a frequent occurrence for example in the western Mediterranean, where a weak low pressure zone over the Gulf of Genoa is sometimes separated from another similar area over north Africa or over the Iberian peninsula by a very weak or non-existent gradient.

If in the short term a weak-to-moderate wind forecast seems reasonable, in the medium term (which might range from a few hours to one or two days) one of the existing depressions might prevail, begin to deepen and radically change wind speeds outlook.

In this case, some help in identifying which low is more likely to develop or deepen may be found in upper level charts, especially 500hPa ones. These charts depict the varying heights over sea level where pressure equals 500hPa.

While their interpretation is beyond the scope of this book, it may be useful to be able to identify a few features which are often found on these charts, which will be occasionally recalled later during the book.

Lines (often called heights or contours) are usually much smoother than surface charts, making their analysis relatively easier; although they represent heights, they can be considered much like isobars: upper level wind will follow their orientation and blow parallel to contours, leaving low heights to its left, and high heights to its right. Their likely influence over developing surface pressure patterns and winds will be indicated in the various parts of the book.

Figure 2.1 and Figure 2.2 show the most typical pressure features of both surface and upper level charts.

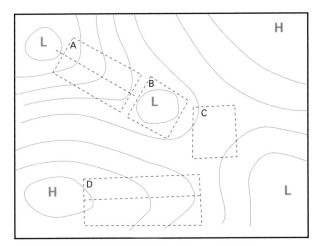

Figure 2.1 Basic surface pressure features
A   Trough and trough axis
B   Secondary low
C   Col/Saddle
D   Ridge and ridge axis

In the case described above of multiple weak lows of relatively equal magnitude, 500hPa charts can give a good indication of the likely development of

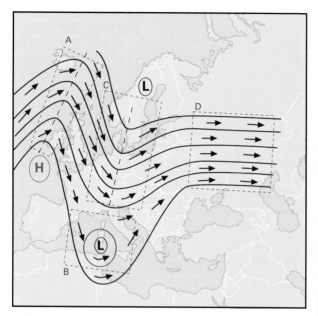

Figure 2.2 Basic upper level contour features
A Ridge and ridge axis
B Cut off low
C Trough and trough axis
D Zonal flow area (ie orientated W to E)

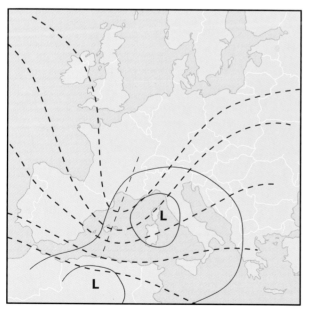

Figure 2.3 500hPa trough and surface low development: the upper level trough is located to the W–NW of a weak Genoa surface low and causes it to deepen

one of them in particular. As low deepening is greatly enhanced by an upper level trough approaching from the west a surface area of weak pressure, the position and likely movement of the trough can give some interesting information.

Figure 2.3 gives an example of an upper level trough approaching from the west, a surface low pressure area located over central Italy, while the depression over northwest Africa is under upper level zonal flow. In this case the first low is much more likely to develop and begin deepening.

Later in this chapter we will examine the most typical low pressure configurations affecting large portions of the Mediterranean Sea, whereas more local ones will be described in the appropriate *Sea Areas* sections.

Heat distribution and variation is another of the basic weather determinants, thermal activity having numberless effects over the weather, from the smallest scale to the planet scale.

A few features of particular interest to the Mediterranean sailor are land-sea breeze systems, thermal lows and fronts or squall lines generated by thermal contrast.

As we have seen in Chapter 1 about Climatology, coastal land-sea breezes are very common during the Mediterranean summers, though much less so during winter. Their behaviour basically follows the textbook rule 'onshore during the day, offshore during the night'; there are slight variations here and there in terms of starting time of the day, wind strength, etc, some of which will be described under the relevant *Sea Areas* sections. They usually provide very pleasant sailing conditions, which make for the reputation of the wonderful Mediterranean sailing summers.

Thermal lows are another common occurrence. They are relatively lower pressure areas developed by intense heating over land, in particular during the daylight hours of hot summer months, especially when the Azores high ridge extends over most of the Mediterranean. Their sizes may be the most varied: from the Spanish thermal low which occupies most of the Iberian peninsula, to smaller ones over the few major Mediterranean islands. They are usually stronger during the day, while at night they sometimes disappear, sometimes just fill moderately. Their end effect is very similar to land-sea breezes, and thermal lows very rarely represent a danger for navigation.

On the other hand, sailors should rather take particular care when more intense thermal contrast takes the form of frontal areas, which may easily originate strong winds to a smaller or larger scale.

An example may be given by fronts of Atlantic origin: when they reach the Mediterranean, their characteristics may be deeply modified by the several mountain chains existing along their path, or by the warmers waters of the sea. Sometimes they weaken and disappear; sometimes they seem to weaken while during the following hours they rapidly deepen, at other times they simply remain stable, hovering over a certain part of the sea. Sometimes they may be fragmented, and accompany the multiple lows distribution described above.

While deep fronts extending vertically through most of the atmosphere usually cross over the mountains with ease, sometimes even accelerate, other shallower fronts may be retarded or vanish, sometimes just to reappear a short time later in an adjacent area.

These characteristics mean than there is always some degree of probability that a front (be it active or decaying) will eventually generate strong winds, so whatever strength they may show on surface charts their presence is a relevant piece of information which should be monitored.

It is also often useful to keep in mind their possible position even after they have disappeared from weather charts, as at a later time they may regain their former strength or even cause new instability developments.

In the following Sections the main types of Mediterranean depressions will be described, while under each *Sea Area* other varieties of more localised lows will be shown.

As each one of them may occur in an extremely variable manner, drawings are quite schematic and represent highly idealised situations: the actual locations of low centres, the extension of low pressure areas, the shape of isobars, etc. will obviously differ to a varying extent from what shown on the drawings, still they should reasonably allow recognizing and following pressure behaviour in the actual world.

Likewise, the various types of depressions may yield more or less manageable weather: as strong wind/gale situations are the main concern for sailors, the text has been aimed at describing the situations which might be most troublesome for navigation.

The section on page 17 of this Chapter will indicate some helpful methods of determining actual wind speed from pressure charts.

BALEARIC SEA DEPRESSIONS

These are low pressure areas located around the East coast of Spain, roughly over the Balearic islands archipelago.

The highest frequency of Baleares depressions occurs in winter, they sometimes happen in autumn and spring, whereas they are quite rare during summer.

Formation and evolution of the low

There usually are two typical situations causing low development over the Baleares.

They can best be examined by looking at surface pressure charts together with 500hPa constant pressure chart.

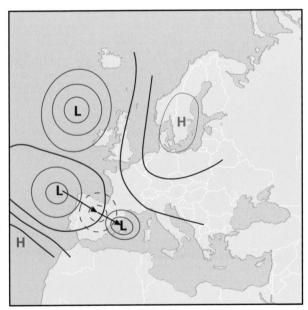

Figure 2.A.1 Typical surface level chart of a Type 1 Balearic low

The large, stable Iceland low has drifted south, reaching an area on the NW of Ireland. The Açores high has moved somewhat south, but a ridge may extend towards the African NW Atlantic coast.

Cold air flows over Spain from the north east, while warm air from north Africa enters the central western Mediterranean.

The 500hPa chart (Figure 2.A.2) shows a strong zonal flow (parallel to latitude lines) southward of 45°N: depressions from the open Atlantic tend to move in a west to east direction.

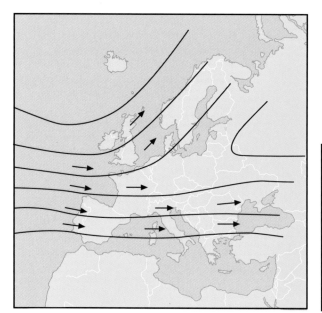

Figure 2.A.2 Typical upper level chart of a Type 1 Balearic low

While they move over Spain, Atlantic depressions are often observed to weaken (sometimes almost disappear from pressure charts): although this might be interpreted as a good sign, the situation must be followed carefully, as this pattern is responsible for about one out of six west Mediterranean lows.

In fact, when the Atlantic low meets the mountain chains of the Iberian peninsula, powerful secondary lows can rapidly develop in the lee of the mountain, over the Balearic islands.

They initially bring southerly winds of gale or strong gale force with even stronger gusts; the usual evolution of their directions is shown in Figure 2.A.3.

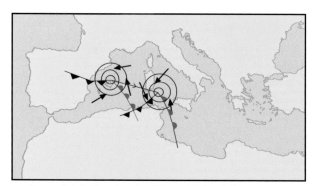

Figure 2.A.3 Usual path of Type 1 Balearic low

The seas build accordingly, and can get very confused after the passage of the front.

The lifecycle of these lows usually lasts three or four days, and their usual path is from the Baleares towards the south of Sardinia, although sometimes they move northeastward towards the south of France where they dissipate or continue their movement across the Alps. Figure 2.A.4.

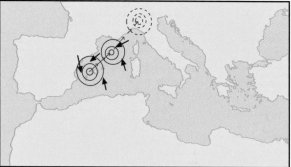

Figure 2.A.4 Alternative path for Type 1 Balearic low

Situation 2. The second typical situation occurs when depressions in the Bay of Biscay are driven southeastward by the upper level flow.

A sometimes complex area of various low pressure centres exists over the UK and central Europe, while the Açores high reaches to the west of Gibraltar. Figure 2.A.5.

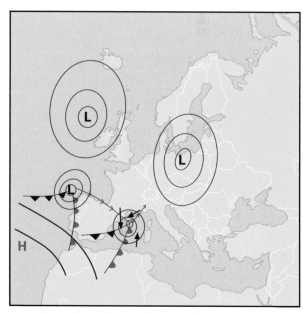

Figure 2.A.5 Type 2 Balearic low at surface level

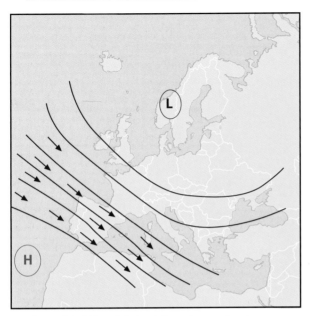

Figure 2.A.6 Type 2 Balearic low at upper level

Depressions from the area NW of Spain cross the Iberian peninsula over or slightly southward of the Pyrenees, then usually slow down and curve towards the southern French Coast. The main effect is strong NE to NW winds along the coast of Spain and southern France. *See Figure 2.A.6 for a 500hPa chart example.*

These low are of relatively shorter duration, but the phenomenon may repeat over several days with new lows following each other along the same path.

GENOA DEPRESSIONS

The Gulf of Genoa is an area where low systems develop with one of the highest frequencies in the entire world.

Various factors are responsible for these formations, the most important being probably the presence of the Alps: northerly flows over the mountain chain increase the likelihood of low development along their concave southern edge; similarly, cold fronts are sometimes blocked by the Alps and help generating depressions to the south, etc.

The Alps, together with a temperature gradient between land and sea indicating thermal differences, the frequent interaction between the polar and subtropical jet streams, and the channelling effects of the various central Mediterranean mountain

chains which tend to accumulate warm air over the area, make the Gulf of Genoa one of the most important weather areas in the Mediterranean.

Genoa low pressure minima are usually centred somewhere in the Gulf, but they may extend into the Po valley and the Gulf of Venice/northern Adriatic. The maximum gradient areas around these lows are not necessarily near the Gulf, but may happen in several different zones, synoptic charts can be useful in determining where the strongest winds are likely.

These depressions can develop all year round. During winter, especially if there is a cold air flow from the north east into the Po valley, the highest frequency occurs in the relatively warmer Gulf of Genoa; whereas during summer (when cold northeasterly air flow is rarer) low centres develop more frequently in the Po valley–northern Adriatic; these lows often move SE along the eastern coast of Italy.

Formation of the low

To ascertain the likelihood of Genoa low formation, watch for the following features:

- A disturbance (front or depression) transits over western France: a lee trough develops in the Gulf of Genoa-Po valley, it may likely become a depression when the disturbance gets nearer to the Gulf of Genoa area.

- Cold air from the north east invades the Po valley. We will see later that in this case the depression is likely to move SE along the west coast of Italy

- A Genoa low is very likely when conditions for the formation of Mistral exist (*see under Mistral section*).

- When a low pressure field covers the western Mediterranean and gradients are weak, two areas of relatively lower pressure are usually found over the Genoa region and over north Africa. In this case one should check the upper level 500hPa chart. If a trough approaches the Gulf of Genoa, a depression is likely to form as described above. If on the contrary the upper level trough transits at lower latitude nearer the north African coast, a depression will form there, and SE to NE gale force winds may develop over the southern Tyrrhenian Sea.

Evolution and movement of the depression

There are three main types of behaviour of Genoa lows.

1. In presence of a strong southwesterly flow in the upper atmosphere, and a ridge of surface high pressure spread over the central Mediterranean, the Genoa low usually drifts NE–NNE towards the Alps, proceeds along the Po valley and eventually crosses the mountain chain toward central Europe. After the main low has left the area, a relatively low pressure area may remain in the Gulf of Genoa region, where new cyclogenesis may take place. This movement happens with the highest frequency during the transition seasons, spring and autumn. With sufficiently deep lows, winds may reach strong gale force.

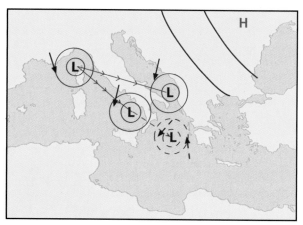

Figure 2.B.2 Genoa low migrating SE when a stable high pressure area is found over the Balkans and Russia

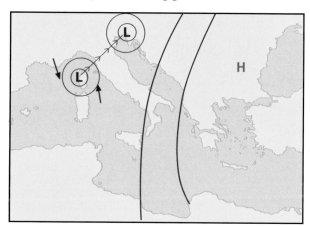

Figure 2.B.1 Genoa low migrating to the NE: a blocking high pressure area is found from the Balkans to the eastern Mediterranean

2. In presence of a strong high pressure area over the Balkans and Turkey, the low cannot proceed to the east and follows a southeasterly path over the Tyrrhenian Sea, or slowly crosses the Italian peninsula and the Apennine.

   Heavy precipitation takes place along the western coast of Italy, and when the low arrives in the southern Tyrrhenian Sea, northeasterly winds often blow at gale or strong gale force, helped by the katabatic effect of the Apennine chain.

   After the main depression has left, a low pressure trough often remains over the Gulf of Genoa-Po valley, in this case new lows can rapidly develop and may follow their predecessors direction. Bad weather can last several days, sometimes as long as a week.

Sometimes these SE migrating lows reach the Sicily area, become stationary and begin filling: in this case watch for a new low to develop over the Ionian Sea, between Sicily and Greek islands.

This Type 2. evolution can occur throughout all the year, although the highest frequency is during summer and early winter (December–January).

3. If the high pressure area extends from the Balkans into the central Mediterranean, the low usually remains stationary.

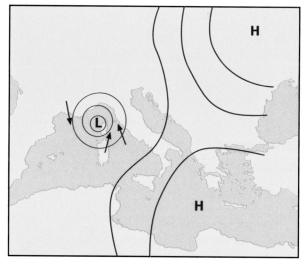

Figure 2.B.3 Stationary Genoa low: a high pressure area extends from the Balkans and Russia region to the eastern Mediterranean, preventing significant movements of the low

This situation is more frequent in the first half of the year. Southerly, moist winds blow to the east of the depression bringing huge areas of precipitation, whereas along the south coast of France winds from the northerly sectors can reach gale and strong gale force. Usually, this low slowly fills in three or four days.

In most cases, Genoa low development is strictly associated with Mistral wind: if Mistral may and does blow locally, the presence of a closed Genoa depression or a low pressure trough will likely spread Mistral over most of the central western Mediterranean. Under the *Mistral Wind* section we will examine more closely their relationship.

NORTH WEST AFRICA (NWA) DEPRESSIONS

Sometimes called Sahara lows, as their name indicates these depressions are generated in northwestern Africa, south of the Atlas mountain chain.

They account for roughly ⅓ of Mediterranean depressions, and are more likely in autumn and spring (roughly one half of total cyclones number during each period); they are rare during summer. Related weather usually lasts three to four days.

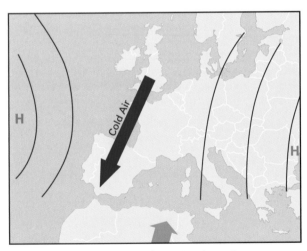

Figure 2.C.1 General NWA formation dynamics

Formation of the low

At surface level, two areas with relatively higher pressure exist west of the Iberian peninsula and over the Balkans: a NE to N flow brings cold air towards north Africa, where it comes in contrast with warm air from the African continent. Figure 2.C.1.

The Atlas mountain chain usually delays the deepening of the low until it has reached the Gulf of Gabes, from where it may enter the central Mediterranean. Sometimes, on the other hand, the low remains stable and does not deepen nor move from its original location over land.

Possibly the most useful indices of NWA development are given by 500hPa upper air charts.

If 500hPa charts show a trough over Spain, and a corresponding southwesterly flow over NW Africa, a deep NWA low is very likely, especially if upper wind speeds are in excess of 50kn.

If a moving upper level trough comes near the area (for example in association with a depression of Atlantic origin moving towards central Europe), deep cyclogenesis usually occurs, and the low usually begins migrating.

If on the other hand the upper level trough is stationary, the Sahara low is not likely to deepen much as it leaves the area. Figure 2.C.2.

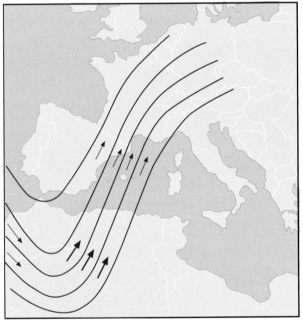

Figure 2.C.2 A 500hPa trough bringing SW flow over northwest Africa: low formation is very likely if upper level winds (bold arrows) are 50kn or stronger

NWA lows can also develop when a long wave trough is oriented NE–SW across the Tyrrhenian Sea, and an upper level cold air centre can be found over Sardinia, Sicily and Tunisia. Often, the subtropical jet stream can be identified over north Africa. Figure 2.C.3.

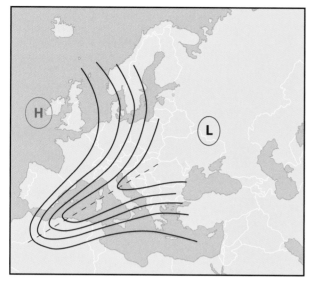

Figure 2.C.3 NE–SW oriented upper level trough

Evolution and movement of the low.

Figure 2.C.4. shows the typical paths of NWA depressions.

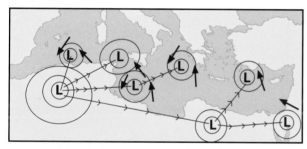

Figure 2.C.4 Typical trajectories of NWA lows

During winter, the most probable tracks are those to the N or NE, while during spring NWA lows tend to follow a more easterly direction.

The typical path of NWA depressions is generally first eastward, south and parallel to the Atlas chain, and then northeast towards the central Mediterranean and Ionian Sea. This is the more likely track during spring.

If the low pressure area over Turkey is 1000hPa or lower, lows can be expected to continue towards this area; if on the other hand the Turkey region only shows a moderate low or even a high pressure, the majority of NWA lows tend to stop and remain stationary over the Ionian Sea.

A secondary, less likely track is followed by some lows (also called Sharav cyclones) whose centre remains over the north African continent while

drifting to the east. They are usually shallow, weak systems developing during spring, which do not last more than one or two days. Sharav lows are usually generated either by:

1. Low pressure on the lee of Atlas mountain, with an upper level trough to the West;

2. Upper level trough and surface level trough over north Africa. Cloudiness of Sharav lows is composed mainly by high and middle level clouds (cirrus and altostratus): if middle level cloudiness increases ahead of the low, these lows may curve NE towards Crete-Asia Minor region, rapidly deepen and cause gale to strong gale force winds in the central eastern Mediterranean.

A final possible track, especially during winter, may occur when upper level SW flow is particularly strong, or is oriented more between S and SW: in this case a secondary low pressure centre may develop on the sea north of the Algerian coast, and drift north-northeastward. This secondary low can be very powerful, but often fills when the original low reaches the Ionian Sea through the Gulf of Gabes.

When the low is deep but is still over land, south of the Atlas mountains, gale to storm force SE to E winds can be expected in the southern Mediterranean, particularly in the strait of Sicily where huge seas may build: these Sirocco winds features will be examined more in depth under the relevant section. Figure 2.C.5.

After the depression has reached the Ionian Sea, the strongest winds tend to blow in the NW sector of the low, especially when 500hPa charts show an area of cold air at their level. Strong NE to NW winds usually blow in the central Mediterranean and Tyrrhenian Sea.

During autumn, when the sea surface is relatively warm, NWA are accompanied by heavy precipitations and thunderstorms, whereas they are weaker when the low develops during spring.

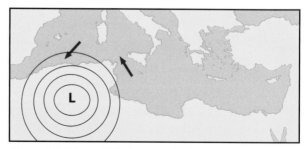

Figure 2.C.5 Deep NWA low over land and related winds

15

IONIAN SEA DEPRESSIONS

The majority of cyclones in the Ionian Sea are either derived from the NWA lows or from the Genoa cyclones.

Evolution and movement of the low

1. A low pressure can develop and deepen in the Ionian if a weak NWA low moves into the area.

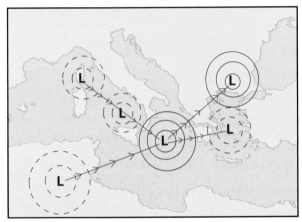

Figure 2.D.1 Ionian sea lows generated by migrating systems

2. It can also be generated by Genoa depressions drifting southeastward towards the Ionian. Figure 2.D.1. These depressions may cross over the Italian boot and reach the Ionian, or they can slow down and become stationary over the south of Italy, in which case a secondary depression often develops over the Ionian.

   In the absence of cold air from the north, Ionian Sea lows usually move NE through Greece and eventually reach the Black Sea.

   If they remain stationary, a secondary low is likely to develop in the Aegean Sea.

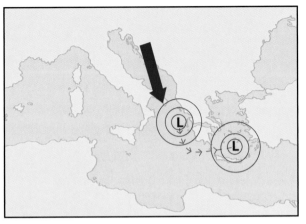

Figure 2.D.2 Ionian Sea lows caused by cold N to NE winds blowing over and out of the Adriatic

3. Low pressure systems can also develop in the North Ionian Sea when there is a strong northerly flow of cold air from the Adriatic Sea.

   Bora winds (*see under Adriatic Sea area section*) usually contribute to deepen these depressions and make them even more powerful. These systems usually drift south (sometimes SW) for a short time, their track is then east towards the southern Aegean Sea.

   From upper level charts, a 500hPa trough with its axis orientated NE–SW across central Italy usually contributes to increase chances of Ionian Sea depressions development.

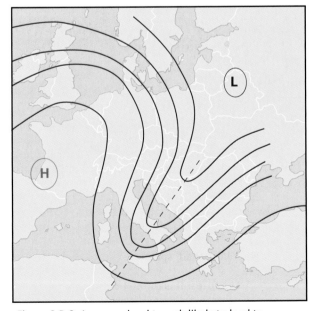

Figure 2.D.3 An upper level trough likely to lead to Ionian Sea low development

WIND SPEED, MIDDLE-SCALE LOCAL EFFECTS AND NUMERICAL FORECASTING

1. Gradient and wind speed

The primary objective of isobaric weather charts is to represent actual or forecast pressure distribution and fronts locations. As wind speed is strictly dependent upon pressure differences, isobaric charts can also be used to determine the likely wind strength over a certain area. This involves measuring pressure gradient, which is simply defined as the pressure variation over a certain distance.

As to direction, wind over the open sea will usually make an angle of 10°–20° with local isobars orientation.

Meteorological theory has found an analytical, numerical relationship between wind speed and pressure gradient: without going into much detail, basically the higher the variation of sea level pressure over a given distance (at a certain time, in a certain area), the higher the expected wind speed. Meteorologists call it geostrophic wind.

On weather charts, a qualitative appreciation of gradient magnitude can be had by looking at isobars packing. As isobars are traced at fixed intervals (usually 4 or 5hPa on commonly available charts), the more they will be packed over a given area, the higher the pressure variation over that distance, the higher the gradient, the stronger the likely wind will be.

Happily, theory allows determining geostrophic wind speed with a lot more accuracy, but as its numerical derivation comes from a precise set of theoretical hypothesis, there are a few modifying elements which must be taken into account before obtaining reasonably accurate values for wind strength at sea level.

1. The first is earth surface friction. Wind speed calculated by gradient theory is related to a height in the atmosphere where wind flow is not influenced by friction with the surface of the earth (typically a height of a few hundred metres): when air moves nearer to the sea surface it is slowed down and its direction is slightly modified to reach the 10°–20° angle with isobars mentioned above. The computed geostrophic wind speed will thus have to be adjusted.

   The first result is the following Table, which takes into account sea surface friction, and shows the average Beaufort wind force to be expected with a given gradient.

Gradient is indicated in number of hPa over degrees of latitude. The distance measured perpendicularly between two adjacent isobars can be directly read in degrees on the latitude grid on the side of the chart. As one degree of latitude equals 60 nautical miles, distances can also be measured in miles and then easily converted into degrees.

Gradient in hPa per Lat °	Gradient in hPa over 1° lat.	Wind Bft
5hPa/1°	5	10
4hPa/1°	4	8/9
10hPa/3°	3·3	7/8
10hPa/4°	2·5	6/7
10hPa/5°	2	5/6
10hPa/7°	1·4	4/5
10hPa/10°	1	3/4

Pressure gradient and expected Beaufort wind force: lower Bft force estimations should be used for gradients measured over the North Mediterranean, higher Bft forces for Southern Mediterranean gradients

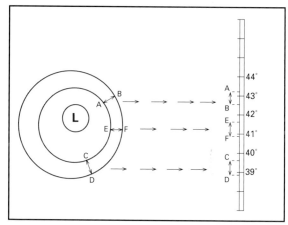

Figure 2.E.1 Dividers may be used to measure the perpendicular distance between isobars, latitude degrees or miles can then be read on the side of the chart

As an approximate guide, if more precise means of measuring are not available:

a. The distance from SW Ibiza to NE Menorca corresponds to about 3°
b. Corsica from N to S covers a bit less than 2°
c. Sardinia from N to S (or Sicily from E to W) covers a bit more than 2°
d. The shortest distance from Sicily to Sardinia is about 2·5°
e. Crete from E to W is slightly more than 2°
f. Cyprus from E to W covers about 2°.

When Beaufort force is given by two numbers (for example 6/7), the lower should be used for gradients placed in the north of the Mediterranean, the higher for gradients computed in its southern part.

If for example we have a chart with 4hPa spaced isobars and we measure a distance of 120 miles between two of them, this equals to 4hPa/2° Lat., which is equivalent to 10hPa/5° Lat. (first Table column), or 2hPa over 1° latitude (second column), so we may expect a 5 Beaufort wind for example with a Balearic depression, or 6Bft with a NWA depression over the southern Ionian Sea.

Very tight gradients like 5hPa/1° usually represent exceptional circumstances, and may quickly change over time: likewise, wind speed related to such gradients may vary below or (worse) above the reported 10Bft.

Spacing of 4hPa isobars in Lat°	Spacing of 4hPa isobars in M	Spacing of 5hPa isobars in Lat°	Spacing of 5hPa isobars in M	Wind Bft
0·8	50	1	60	10
1	60	1·25	75	8/9
1·2	70	1·5	90	7/8
1·6	100	2	120	6/7
2	120	2·5	150	5/6
2·8	170	3·5	210	4/5
4	240	5	300	3/4

Isobars spacing and expected Beaufort wind force

The second Table gives the same information, it simply shows the expected Beaufort force depending on spacing (both in M and latitude degrees) between isobars drawn every 4hPa or isobars drawn every 5hPa, as they usually are in commonly available charts.

With this second table, the two 4hPa-spaced isobars of the example above would show a distance of 2°, hence again 5/6Bft.

To further refine this estimation, the Beaufort force values obtained from the Tables above may have to be modified by the following other factors, if applicable.

2. Air stability. If cold air flows over warm water an unstable situation develops: the cold, heavier air will tend to sink towards the water, while the warm, lighter air layer over the sea will have a tendency to rise. A difference between the temperatures of air and water of 5°C begins to be meaningful, 10°C or more is a sign of important instability.

Depending on the degree of instability, one or two Beaufort notches should be added to the average wind speed derived from the Table above.

Another consequence of instability is wind turbulence, which translates into possible gusts from 20–30% up to 50% stronger than gradient average wind speed. As for wind direction, it may be interesting to know that unstable air tends to blow more parallel to isobars.

Examples of instability are outbreaks of cold air from continental Europe over the Mediterranean, or cold air inflows after the passage of cold fronts.

If on the other hand a warm wind blows over relatively colder water, the situation will be stable. Again, an air-water temperature difference of 5°C indicates good stability, 10°C or above is a sign of very stable air. Depending on the degree of stability, one or two Beaufort notches should be subtracted from the wind speed derived from the Table.

It should be noticed that stable air tends to move more directly towards the centre of the depression, making a greater angle with isobars.

An example of a stable situation is given by sirocco winds, usually much warmer than the sea surface; extended stratus clouds are another common indication of stability in the atmosphere.

Summing up, air stability is quite an important factor as it can greatly modify the likely wind speed associated with a given gradient. As an example, the same pressure gradient might as well generate a force 7/8 gregale (due to higher air instability) or a force 5/6 sirocco (because of higher air stability).

3. Isobars curvature: a given gradient will yield a higher wind when isobars follow the contour of a high pressure area, i.e. when winds tend to rotate clockwise; on the contrary wind speed will be lower when it rotates anticlockwise, like the flow around a depression.

Figure 2.E.2. shows how a given gradient (isobar spacing) can yield different wind speeds depending on isobars curvature, and the average wind angle with isobars.

One or two Beaufort notches should be added respectively in cases of moderate or strong anticyclonic curvature. One Beaufort notch should be subtracted in cases of strong cyclonic curvature.

4. Uneven pressure distribution: as weather charts depict pressure distribution by means of equally spaced isobars (usually four or five hPa), the precision of gradient measurement will be limited by the available isobars spacing. *Figure 2.E.3*

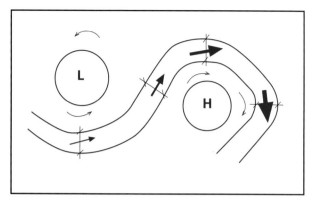

Figure 2.E.2 Isobars curvature and expected wind force: weaker winds are associated with cyclonic curvature (left), stronger winds with isobars with anticyclonic curvature (right)

If for example the 1004 isobar and the 1008 isobar are separated by a distance equal to 2·5° latitude, gradient will be 4hPa/2·5°; this is roughly equal to the 10hPa/7° gradient of the table, which gives an expected wind speed of 5 Beaufort (supposing no isobars curvature and neutral air, neither stable nor unstable). This is the best estimation we can infer from the chart.

In reality, depending on the characteristics of atmospheric flows, etc, pressure may vary in a non uniform way between the two 1008 and 1004 isobars.

The same situation analysed on a more detailed chart (say one with isobars spaced every 1hPa) might show for example the 1006, 1007 and 1008 isobars closely packed together, with the 1004 and 1005 slightly more apart. Obviously the effective gradient will be greater where isobars are nearer to each other, and stronger winds are to be expected; and obviously

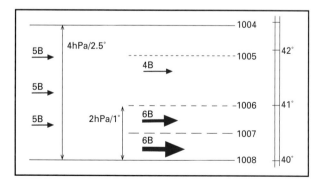

Figure 2.E.3 Uneven pressure distribution and wind strength: if for example wind force from a given gradient is expected at 5Bft (left), uneven pressure distribution may generate areas of 4Bft and 6Bft winds (right)

winds will be lower than expected around the 1006/1004 isobars area.

The degree of precision of wind speed estimates will depend upon the amount of details shown by the available weather charts.

Although no hard and fast rule can be given, with the most commonly available charts (either 4 or 5hPa isobar spacing), serious consideration should be given to gradients equal or higher than 10hPa over 4° latitude, or in other terms if the distance between 4hPa spaced isobars is 1·5° or lower, or if the distance between 5hPa spaced isobars is 2° or lower.

2. Middle scale local effects

With the adjustments indicated above, reasonably accurate wind speeds can be calculated for areas where the flow of air is relatively free and does not meet significant obstacles.

Pressure gradients measured in depressions over Mediterranean open sea areas usually give accurate wind estimations, pretty much like those measured in lows in the middle of the ocean.

But once again, the Mediterranean Sea excels with anomalies.

The important peculiarities of this basin (mountain chains, valleys, islands, peninsulas, capes, straits, etc) imply that in certain areas air may find it more difficult to adjust to pressure differences; in these cases the Beaufort strength obtained by the gradient method described above should be more considered a good starting point in wind speed estimations, rather than a final result.

As modifications in wind strength may be caused by a very vast array of local causes, we will concentrate on the most important ones, whose effects can usually be felt at least over a few tens of miles.

When possible, a qualitative appraisal of the likely smaller scale local effects should be made.

Mountains

A surface wind blowing with some angle of incidence (from 20°–30° to almost perpendicularly) against a sufficiently high mountainous barrier will likely be unable to freely jump over the relief, and its direction will be deflected in a direction more or less parallel to the obstacle. This phenomenon may usually be felt up to a distance of 30–50 miles from the coast.

At the same time, pressure to the windward and leeward sides of the obstacle will be modified, obviously bringing a shift in isobars orientation. To the windward side pressure will tend to rise, while to the leeward side a lower pressure area will usually

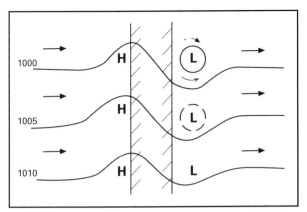

Figure 2.E.4 Isobar shape modification over a mountain barrier: a ridge forms to windward, and a trough or even closed low develops to leeward

form. More often the obstacle will induce a lee trough development, while at times it may even create a closed low, in which case winds will be weaker where they oppose the general flow.

The more stable the air and the higher the obstacle, the more important this effect will be.

As an example, these isobars modifications can occur over the biggest islands (like Sardinia, Crete, etc), or at a larger scale through the Apennine mountains; in the *Winds* and *Sea Areas Chapter* several examples of lee troughs or lows development will be given.

When the new direction taken by the wind forces air to flow from higher pressures to lower pressures, wind speed will be greatly accelerated.

When on the other hand wind flow has a lower incidence angle with the obstacle, isobars will likely be more parallel to the mountain and wind acceleration will be less significant. Figure 2.E.5.

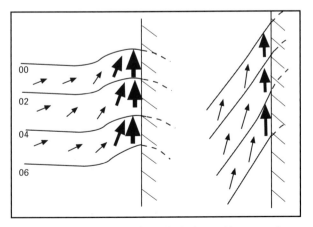

Figure 2.E.5 Isobars angle and wind speed increase: the narrower the angle, the lower the wind speed increase

A particular case of potential rapid strong wind development occurs when a cold front nears a mountainous coast. Figure 2.E.6.

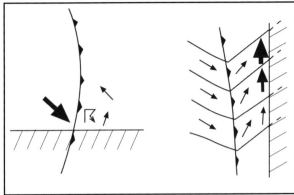

Figure 2.E.6 Cold fronts and coastal mountains. Left: front perpendicular to the coast; right: approaching front with a small angle of incidence to the relief

If the front is more or less perpendicular to the relief, a quick wind increase may be experienced over the sea around their intersection: it usually does not last long but can be violent nonetheless; if thermal contrast is particularly strong, violent thunderstorms may as well develop.

If the front approaches more or less parallel to the mountainous coast, winds are likely to be accelerated all over a relatively wider area, often adding one or two Beaufort notches to theoretical wind speeds calculated as above, especially around the area of relatively lower pressure.

The front does not necessarily need to be very active to cause this kind of phenomena. Indeed, in the Mediterranean it is not unlikely that weak cold fronts, having almost disappeared from weather charts, suddenly regain strength and cause quick heavy winds episodes. For this reason, it is always prudent to follow the movement of fronts, squall or disturbance lines indicated by the charts, and consider their hypothetical evolution during one or two days even after they have disappeared from the map.

Channelling effect

Another common effect is wind acceleration in channels. This is also known as Venturi or funnelling effect, and is a common feature in the many Mediterranean existing straits and channels.

Wind flow approaching a strait will be forced to converge towards its axis, thereby increasing pressure on the windward side; to the lee of the

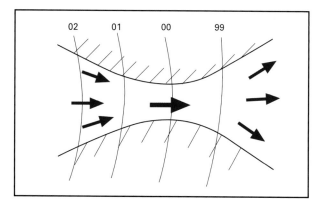

Figure 2.E.7 Channelling effect: wind speed increases can be found in the narrowest part and downwind of the strait

channel, wind flow will likely spread and diverge, causing drops in pressure. The global result is a marked increase in wind speed in the strait. *(See the Winds and Sea Area chapters for more examples of local channelling effects.)*

Depending on the situation, wind strengths in a strait may range from one to three Beaufort notches higher than in the surrounding areas. A similar effect can be found at the mouth of the valleys opening to the sea.

Corner effect

Capes are another geographic feature which usually modifies wind speed and direction.

When wind flow is forced to rotate around a corner, its direction tends to follow the orientation of the coast (much like when meeting a mountain, as described above), while its speed is usually increased.

The effect is somewhat different if the resulting rotation is cyclonic or anticyclonic.

a. Cyclonic rotation: in this case, similarly to what happens with geostrophic wind with cyclonically

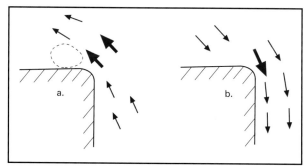

Figure 2.E.8 Corner effect: cyclonic (left) and anticyclonic rotation (right)

curved isobars, wind will be accelerated around the cape, while a region of decreased strength will develop in the immediate lee of the cape (circled area).

b. Anticyclonic rotation: again, similarly to gradient wind resulting from clockwise oriented isobars, speed will likely be greater and be spread throughout the area.

3. Additional forecasting aids

It is important to remind once again that especially while sailing in the Mediterranean, it is always recommended to follow as much as possible the evolution of the weather.

While onboard, regularly recording barometric pressure can provide an easy way of detecting worsening weather, or at least be warned of the possibility of strong winds development.

Unfortunately, it is not always true the other way around: there are many occurrences of strong winds with almost no local pressure variations *(see the Winds and Sea Areas chapters for more details)*. Still, pressure recording being one of the easiest tasks onboard, the following remarks can be of some interest.

a. Pressure daily oscillation

In the absence of other modifying factors, pressure shows a cyclical oscillation during the day. There are usually two maxima, at 1000LT and 2200LT, and two minima at around 0400LT and 1600LT. This phenomenon is quite noticeable at low latitudes and in the Tropics, where it has a remarkable regularity, with amplitudes up to a few hPa.

In the Mediterranean, depending on location, this oscillation may have different characteristics. Sometimes its maxima and minima occur at different times of the day, sometimes the amplitude is 1 or 2hPa, sometimes 3 (or even more where thermal factors are particularly strong), other times it is barely noticeable and the oscillation is practically inexistent.

However, the characteristics of the oscillation for a given location are often rather stable.

This is usually most evident during the nice summer days, when overall pressure often tends to remain high and stable during several days and this barometric tide, if it exists, can easily be revealed by keeping a written track of hourly or three-hourly pressure changes during one or two days.

Once a certain regularity of the daily oscillation has been identified, any significant change should be treated with suspicion.

Suppose having found that in a given place the oscillation follows the typical pattern described above: if during the following days the barometer remains stable or even drops in the early morning or during the late afternoon (instead of showing a small rise as the typical barometric tide would suggest), it may be considered a warning sign of a possible change in pressure tendency which is slowly taking place.

b. Pressure hourly variations

Usually, a decrease in pressure over time means that the weather is likely to deteriorate: this is a very raw barometric guidance, usually based on the fact that a depression is approaching the sailing area.

The drop (or rise) in hPa over a certain time interval which can be measured at a given place depends on several factors, mainly the speed of the pressure system (usually a low), its evolution (if it is deepening of filling), and the relative speed of the boat, so again there is no strict rule allowing to automatically determine wind speed, as it exists between gradient and geostrophic wind.

However, for a cruising boat with an average speed, a drop of 4–5hPa over six hours should not be disregarded, even if winds might not blow much over 15 knots. A drop of 3hPa over 3 hours might mean something stronger, roughly around 20–25 knots. A drop of 3hPa over one hour is definitely something to be taken more seriously, with winds possibly reaching gale or strong gale force. A drop of more than 5hPa over one hour almost surely heralds exceptionally strong wind conditions.

Again, the opposite is often not true: strong winds can be experienced even when local pressure does not move at all, Mistral wind being a typical example (*see the relevant section for more details*).

c. Daily pressure drops

Another helpful warning sign of changing conditions in most areas of the Mediterranean, especially when no particular system prevails and weather appears rather stable, is a slow barometric drop: pressure falls by more than 5–7hPa a day should always be considered with suspicion, as more powerful phenomena may well develop later.

d. Absolute pressure value

Finally, while strong winds may come with the most varied pressure values and distributions, as a general rule particular care should be taken with depressions whose centre shows a pressure lower than 1000 hPa.

Obviously, if any of these barometric patterns is experienced together with modifications in other weather elements (cirrus clouds, distant cumulonimbus development, oncoming swell, etc), the forecast of worsening conditions should be given a higher degree of confidence. The more elements converge towards a particular weather scenario, the more likely it should be considered.

4. Forecast charts

Today, the vast majority of pressure charts describing a situation at a given moment in the future are built with the help of complex numerical models which are often run several times a day, the computer output is usually rearranged by the human intervention of expert forecasters before the product is eventually made available to the public.

While the characteristics of these models are far beyond the scope of this book, it is important to make a distinction between two broad model categories which are of interest to cruisers: synoptic or global scale models, and meso-scale or L.A.M. Limited Area Models.

First, a distinction between different meteorological features should be made. Depending on their extension over time and over space, weather elements are usually divided into four main categories.

a. Earth scale: these are mainly related to planetary patterns, have a duration of several months (like for example seasonal patterns), and extend over several thousand miles; one typical phenomenon is the Asian monsoon wind, caused by interacting global scale factors like the Indian Ocean and the Asian continent land mass.

b. Large scale: also called synoptic scale, these phenomena usually span over a few days, and usually cover several hundred miles extension. Examples are depressions, fronts, etc. A synoptic scale factor influencing cyclogenesis in the Mediterranean is for example the Alps mountain chain.

c. Meso scale: these usually develop over a few tens of miles, and usually last up to a day. Land-sea breeze systems or local wind modifications due to orographic effects are examples of meso scale weather features.

d. Small scale: these are mainly local occurrences, whose life span is often of a few hours, and which cover an area just a few miles wide, like for example wind shelter on the lee of a small island.

Naturally, actual weather at a given moment and location will be determined by the combination and interaction of all these different scale elements and processes.

This distinction is not only academic; the capacity to understand the predominating temporal and spatial scale of current weather characteristics may be very useful for cruisers. Suppose to be placed all of a sudden in the middle of a gale with pouring rain: it is quite a different thing to know to be sailing in a small scale thunderstorm which will likely end in a couple of hours, or being in the middle of a stationary depression, possibly lasting for one or two days.

But again, unlike the open ocean, things are not that easy in the Mediterranean.

The higher complexity of the region on one side increases the importance of the meso scale factors component (which is more difficult to integrate in forecasting models), on the other side it greatly deepens the interactions between factors of various scale, often making it difficult to distinguish between them, which in turn translates in an increased complexity for weather forecasting.

Going back to models, it may be said that each of the two broad categories mentioned above (global and LAM/meso-scale) represents a privileged viewing point over weather elements of the corresponding scale.

The structure of every single numerical model is of course different, and their equation systems may take into account different sets of variables from different spatial and temporal scales, but with a bit of simplification it may be said that one type of models is mainly concentrated over global/synoptic aspects, the other mainly over meso-scale aspects.

The most important model output for cruisers is of course the weather chart.

Synoptic model

Synoptic model charts are the most widely available: many forecast pressure charts issued by meteorological offices are produced by models of this type, they are those usually printed on newspapers, shown on TV weather broadcasts, etc.

As their name states, they are built to describe the actual situation or optimize forecasting at synoptic scale: they usually cover substantial portions of whole continents (for example an area spanning from the near Atlantic to north Africa/Middle East to north of Scandinavia), showing stable or developing pressure areas, movement of fronts or major disturbance lines, etc.

These models can be run to produce forecast weather charts up to several days in the future, obviously with a varying degree of confidence in the final product.

Besides pressure charts, computers can also automatically generate wind field charts from actual or forecast pressure distributions, usually as a grid of equally spaced arrows indicating speed and direction.

While this is certainly very interesting, a few comments are appropriate.

a. Wind field charts will mainly reflect isobars orientation and spacing at synoptic level, so to have a better approximation of the real world, wind values shown by the chart should integrate (at least) the corrections indicated earlier in this Chapter when discussing the influence of local factors.

b. Notwithstanding point a. synoptic wind fields will sometimes 'miss' or underestimate the intensity of local phenomena like mistral or bora, where orographic factors play an important role; like they would probably miss quickly developing local phenomena like thunderstorms, etc.

c. Synoptic wind fields often underestimate wind speeds in specific situations, namely under squall lines, in cold sectors of frontal passages, or in general in areas of high air instability,

d. Synoptic wind fields are usually smoothed and local peaks often averaged out: if for example a forecast wind field chart is built with a 12 hour interval over a grid of 1° and wind arrows are accordingly shown with the same spacing, it is likely that wind arrows have been computed by smoothing three or four latitude degrees data. This in turn means that: 1) as wind speed distribution may be far from uniform, there can be a lot of uncertainty in inferring wind speed or direction at a point halfway between two arrows of the same chart; or 2) there may also be a lot of uncertainty in inferring wind speed or direction at a given location at time h+6 hours, i.e. halfway between the two 12-hour spaced charts.

In terms of sailing and passage planning, a 5Bft wind evenly spread over 60M is quite different from having 3Bft on one extreme of the area, and 8Bft at the other extreme; or similarly beginning a passage with 3Bft and ending up with 40 knots twelve hour later, rather than enjoying a broad reach with 20 knots for the full length. These are of course extreme examples, just to suggest that proper caution is advisable when dealing with these products.

Additional indications about global-synoptic model interpretation will be given under the Weather information Appendix when discussing GRIB files.

Models belonging to this family include the US GFS Global Forecast System which is widely used by several weather forecast providers, the Global model used by the Met Office to prepare its largest pressure charts, Meteo France ARPEGE model, etc.

LAM – Meso-scale models

LAM - Meso-scale models on the other hand, are made by sets of equations and variables which allow taking into account also smaller scale features: being built over grids of points with spacings of just a few nautical miles or even lower, their output charts are a lot more detailed.

Meso-scale charts may indicate and quantify to a great detail the importance of modifications of pressure and wind fields at local level. They will usually show isobars and wind modifications over mountains and islands, near the various orographic features, their likely evolution during the day, etc.

Here are a couple of examples of the kind of detail that can be reached by high resolution models.

The first one is a pressure chart over the Aegean from the Greek Met office: isobars are quite dense as they have a 1-hPa spacing and allow to see a few of the middle-scale local effects described on page 19. There is a remarkable effect of Crete island over isobars orientation, a small low pressure is developing over Rhodes, some gradient with channelling effect exists in the Corinth Sea and the Dardanelles, etc. There is comparatively a lot of information, as a corresponding global scale chart would probably have shown only the two 1012 and 1008 isobars.

The second is a high resolution LAM model wind charts around Sardinia, note the density of the grid: every point is computed taking into account an enormous number of variables, and integrates the physical characteristics of its exact location.

Considering that besides the spatial density of their data these forecast charts may often be built at one hour intervals, LAM appear as very powerful tools.

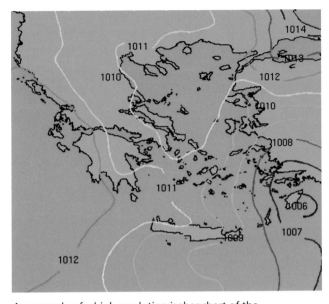

An example of a high resolution isobar chart of the Aegean sea

Hellenic Center for Marine Research

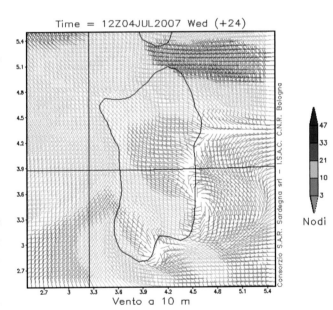

An example of a high resolution wind chart of Sardinia
Consorzio SAR Sardegna

Models of this type include the HIRLAM High Resolution Limited Area Model, jointly developed by several European countries' meteorological offices, Aladin (developed by Meteo France in conjunction with other European and North African countries) and the soon to be released very high resolution Arome model, the Greek Poseidon model (based on University of Belgrad / US ETA model), and other LAM operated by some Italian Universities (e.g. BOLAM, LAMMA, etc)

Now the obvious question: which works best?

Data obtained from any kind of model will always be the result of mathematical equations, so obviously never immune from errors.

At first sight the impressive detail given by LAM charts looks very appealing for cruiser on slow-moving sailboats, and one might question why bother with global scale models.

The answer lays in the conceptual relationship between the two model categories.

First of all there is a technical reason: to build a LAM grid output, meteorologists have to initialize the meso-scale model with a starting large scale environment, i.e. the LAM needs a series of physical data describing in numerical terms what are the conditions around and over the Limited Area, its equations will then build high resolution charts from this starting set of information.

Most LAM take this coarser starting data from the global model, apply it to the Limited Area characteristics, and eventually obtain the kind of details as seen above. Simply said, local models usually need global data to produce local data.

But the necessity of a global model is not only related to the initialization of the LAM; there is another reason of more interest to sailors. Suppose a moving depression whose trajectory will cross the Limited Area at some time in the future: the LAM would not 'see' the depression until it is reflected by the synoptic data of the contour which is used to run the LAM, and until this happens medium term forecasts from the Limited Area model might obviously be very inaccurate, no matter how detailed they are. As soon as a new 'run' of the model integrates the coming depression in the global environment used by the LAM, the medium term forecast would obviously be very different from the previous one, and probably more accurate.

For this reason, and because of the mathematical relationship existing between the two types of models, forecasting with LAM should be (and usually is) kept to a limited time horizon, inversely related to the grid spacing.

Beyond a forecasting horizon of a certain amount of hours, LAM tend to lose their effectiveness and lose most of their interest in favour of synoptic models (especially as the latter use a fraction of the computing power).

As of today, it is usually suggested that LAM having a 10nm grid spacing usually 'converge' towards basic synoptic models beyond 48/72 hours, those with 5M spacing retain their identity up to no more than 36/48 hours, those with one or two nautical miles grid should be used with horizons of 24, 36 hours at most. In cases of strong uncertainty (for example various models giving radically different outputs) it is best to err on the safe side and halve the above forecasting intervals.

Summing up, LAM and global models are both effective at describing two different but complementary aspects of the same reality at some point in the future, so whenever possible output charts from different categories of models should be examined together.

In other words, and given the Mediterranean peculiarities, before relying on a model forecast (especially those often offered by subscription services) it is very important to ascertain from which type of model data is derived, and consider the suitability of the related model category to the intended navigation. A few hour hop between two Greek islands might well take advantage of a correct timing given by a high resolution model, but a two, three day open water passage from southern Aegean to Sicily would better be planned with a synoptic model forecast.

The *Appendix* on *Weather Forecasts* indicates several ways of getting weather forecast from different sources, from both synoptic and meso-scale models, and separately lists the major producer of high resolution charts.

3. Winds

MEDITERRANEAN WINDS

As we have seen, weather wise the Mediterranean is far from being a uniform area: mountains, valleys, deserts, plateaus, islands etc contribute to differentiate each small Mediterranean area from the others, each one having its own particular features.

This is of course reflected by the variety of winds affecting the area. Many of these winds have a local name, and sometimes one particular wind can be known under different local names, as is the case of sirocco, whose name varies along the north African shore.

To add to the confusion, a same given name is often used in two or more different areas, and related to different types of winds: for example, tramontane is the name given to a mistral-like northwesterly wind along the SW coast of France, but also that of a NE katabatic wind along the western coast of Italy.

Regardless of all local name varieties, the most relevant winds will be described in a hopefully organic way, in order to make them clearly identifiable however they may be locally labelled.

Figure 3.A.1. depicts some of the most common names given to local winds.

Bora a cold katabatic northeasterly wind originated from the Karst mountains and Dalmatian Alps, along the eastern coast of Italy, which can affect the whole of the Adriatic and part of the Ionian Sea. (*See Bora section for more details.*)

Cers a name often given to mistral along the SW coast of France and NE coast of Spain. It is a violent and gusty wind, often cold in winter and hot in summer, usually associated with clear skies. (*See Mistral section for more details*).

Chergui a name given in northern Morocco to a E to SE dry wind, usually warm during summer and cold in winter. It is usually caused by a high pressure area in the Mediterranean, with isobars parallel to the coast.

Figure 3.A.1 Mediterranean winds

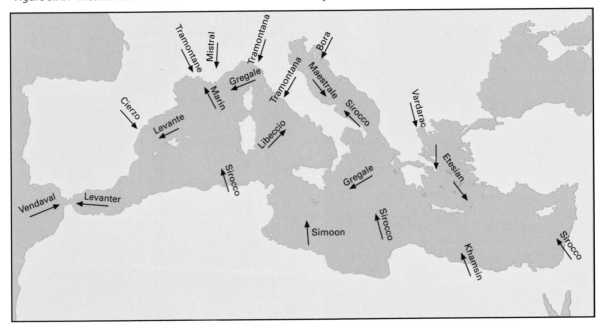

Chili a warm, dry sirocco-like Tunisian wind.

Cierzo a name given to a NW, Mistral-like wind blowing along the valley of river Ebro. It is mainly an autumn and early winter wind.

Dusenwind a strong E to NE wind blowing from the Black Sea into the Aegean through the Bosphorus and Dardanelles Straits. It is usually caused by a high pressure area over the Black Sea.

Etesian a periodic monsoon-like NE to NW summer wind, usually blowing over the Aegean Sea but sometimes affecting adjacent areas. The same wind is often called Meltemi. *(See the Aegean Sea section for more details.)*

Ghibli a very common name for various desert winds (other spellings are gibla, chibli, gebli, gibleh, gibli, kibli, etc). Its name means 'the direction in which one turns', i.e., the traditional direction of Mecca, but locally the wind may come from a different direction.

Gregale a strong northeasterly wind usually occurring during winter over the central and western Mediterranean. *(See Gregale section for more details).*

Khamsin a hot, dry desert wind blowing from the S or SE over the Red Sea and northern Egypt. Other common spellings are camsin, chamsin, kansin, khamasseen, khemsin. Khamsin meaning fifty in Arabic, its name derives from its higher frequency during the fifty days following spring equinox.

Levante a NE to SE wind occurring over the western Mediterranean, from the south of France to Gibraltar. Also called Levanter near the Strait of Gibraltar. *(See Levante section for more details.)*

Leveche a Spanish name for a hot, dusty SE to SW sirocco-like wind.

Libeccio an Italian name for a W to SW wind in the Tyrrhenian area. It can happen all year, but is usually more violent during winter.

Liberator a less common name for western winds at Gibraltar.

Lips name given to hot, sirocco-like winds in the Gulf of Athens.

Maestro, or Maestrale a NW, fine weather breeze-like wind blowing over the Adriatic Sea, but also Corsica and Sardinia, especially during summer.

Mamatele a NW hot wind blowing over Sicily and Malta, but of much lesser strength than mistral.

Marin a S to SE warm, moist wind blowing along the south coast of France. It may blow to strong gale force when a depression from Spain increases the pressure gradient from the south of France towards Corsica and Sardinia.

Meltemi (or Meltem) the Turkish name for Etesian winds. It also indicates a strong E to NE summer winds occurring in the western Black Sea. *(See the Aegean Sea section for more details).*

Mistral a strong to violent wind from the northerly sectors blowing in the central western Mediterranean. *(See Mistral section for more details).*

Poniente, or Ponente generally, a western wind of the Mediterranean. Over the SE coast of France and Corsica it is often called Ponant, and tends to blow from the SW; during summer it is usually not stronger than 4/5Bft.

Simoon a name with many local variants given to a strong, very hot, dry and dusty wind blowing from the Arabian desert, towards all the south and southeastern rim of the Mediterranean.

Siffanto a SW strong wind of the south Adriatic.

Sirocco, or Scirocco a name used in several areas of the Mediterranean, usually to refer to a southern quadrants wind. It is dry along the north coast of Africa, but becomes moist and rainy while travelling northward. Local variants are xaroco (Portugal), jaloque or xaloque (Spain), and xaloc or xalock (SE Spain). *(See Sirocco section for more details.)*

Solano a variant of the Leveche, the name indicates a SE, usually moisty breeze along the SE coast of Spain, usually announced by a coloured cloud strip appearing on the southern horizon.

Tramontana a name used in various areas, usually to indicate a cold N to NE wind. It usually blows over the north and western coast of Italy, Corsica, SW coast of Spain, Balearic islands and SE coast of Spain.

Vardarac also called Vardar, a NW wind blowing in the northern Aegean from the Vardar river valley into the Thessaloniki Gulf; it generally blows in winter, and lasts a couple of days.

Vendaval a S to SW wind occurring in the Alboran Sea and Gibraltar area. Often of gale to strong gale force, it is accompanied by heavy precipitation and thunderstorms.

MISTRAL

The mistral is a strong, cold wind blowing from a NE to NW direction in the western central Mediterranean, in particular along the south coast of France. Figure 3.B.1.

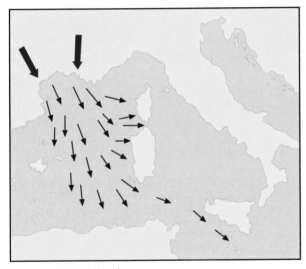

Figure 3.B.1 Mistral area

When localized, mistral may affect only a relatively small sea band along the southern coast of France, whereas when widespread it can have an influence over most of the western half of the Mediterranean, as far as northern Africa and Malta.

It often blows 8/9Bft, with even stronger gusts.

It generally lasts several days; in some cases it may intermittently show short periods with a reduced intensity, after which it may blow again at its strongest.

Several factors contribute to the development and strength of mistral.

a. The existence of a west to east pressure gradient in the south of France, with lower pressure to the east, and higher pressure to the West, creating a Northerly air flow over southern France.

b. The orographic configuration of the coast. When transiting over the southern half of France, the cold air flow is accelerated in two ways:

1. by moving downward from the mountains, wind accelerates when reaching the sea; and
2. by the various gaps existing in the mountain relief (Rhône valley, Toulouse/Carcassonne gap, etc), which channel the flow and contribute to accelerate it even more.

The strongest mistral spells usually occur when isobars form an angle of 30° with the valleys orientations.

c. The increase in wind speed offshore, as the air mass flowing over the sea encounters less friction in respect to land.

Mistral is strictly related to Genoa depressions: if the northwestern flow is strong enough, it will eventually generate a pool of warm air south of the mountain chain, and a Genoa low will likely develop. The more the Genoa depression deepens, the stronger the mistral will be; when the Genoa low migrates away from its area of origin, mistral will likely end. See later in the text for more details about their relationship.

Formation and forecasting

There are three typical 500hPa patterns which can lead to the development of mistral; it can obviously be very useful to recognize them on actual or forecast upper level charts.

1. A ridge on the west of the British isles, followed by a trough over central Europe. This combination produces a strong northwesterly flow over France. Figure 3.B.2.

With upper wind speeds over southern France of 50kn or above mistral is almost certain, with lower speeds or with the NW flow farther east or west of the circled area there is a somewhat lower degree of confidence.

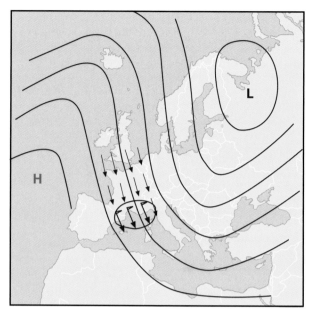

Figure 3.B.2 500hPa pattern for Type 1 mistral: winds of 50kn or above around the South of France (circled area) are a very good indication of a strong mistral

2. A ridge extending towards the NE, over northern Europe, while southern Europe and the Mediterranean is under a trough from the Siberian region. Figure 3.B.3.

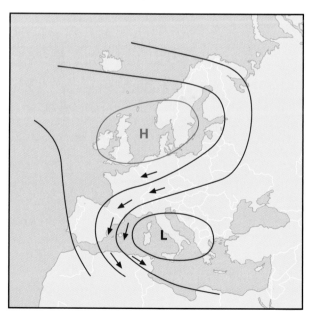

Figure 3.B.3 500hPa pattern for Type 2 mistral

3. Zonal flow over Europe. 500hPa contours are roughly parallel to latitude lines, and mid-atmosphere flow tends to be oriented west - east.

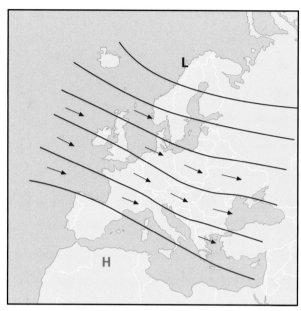

Figure 3.B.4 500hPa pattern for Type 3 mistral: zonal (mainly west to east) flow over Europe

As shown in Figure 3.B.2., in an upper level situation of Type 1 strong mistral is very likely to develop when an upper level trough extends over the Mediterranean and associated 500hPa winds of northerly to westerly origin towards the Golfe du Lion have a speed of over 50 knots. A slightly different location or speed of the upper winds will slightly reduce the degree of confidence of mistral onset.

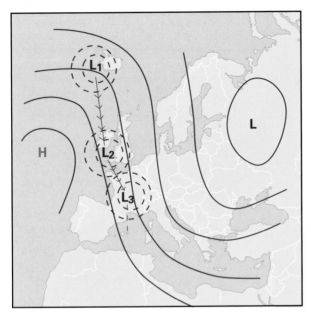

Figure 3.B.5 Typical surface chart with a Type 1 mistral: a low pressure area migrates SE from around Iceland, driven by the upper level flow

Meanwhile, at surface level, whenever a low (L_1) is present around the south of Iceland (Figure 3.B.5.), the situation should be closely followed as this can give a couple of days warning of mistral conditions: the upper level flow might force the depression to migrate southeastward to the UK (L_2) during the following day, and when eventually its trough reaches the SW coast of France (L_3) mistral will

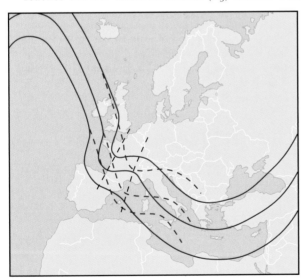

Figure 3.B.6 Mistral is very likely when the axis of a small upper level trough accompanying the surface low transits over SW France

start. On upper level charts (Figure 3.B.6.), the same phenomenon is likely to be reflected by a smaller scale trough drifting to the SE with the large scale flow: another excellent sign of mistral start is the trough axis transiting over SW France.

Two other situations can give useful advance warning signs of a Type 1 oncoming mistral.

In the first (Figure 3.B.7.), upper level winds over the British Isles are northwesterly, with a speed of 50kn or greater.

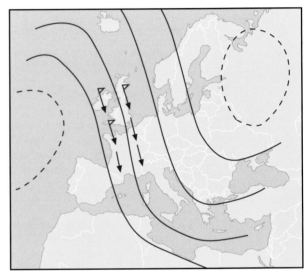

Figure 3.B.7 Type 1 mistral is likely when NW upper level winds over the UK have a speed of 50kn or greater

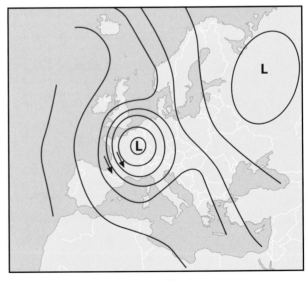

Figure 3.B.8 A cut-off upper level low generates a northwesterly flow over the South of France

In the second (Figure 3.B.8.), a cut-off low at 500hPa is over NE France and generates an upper level NW flow over the south coast of France.

In association with upper level features of Type (2), mistral is likely to be preceded one day earlier by a 500hPa trough moving over the south coast of France, and the development of a Genoa surface depression (dashed lines).

Mistral will likely start when 500hPa wind direction over Bordeaux is from the northern quadrant (NE to NW) as the upper level trough transits over southern France. Figure 3.B.9.

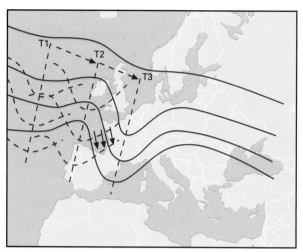

Figure 3.B.10 Type 3 mistral: upper level large scale zonal flow over Europe: small scale troughs follow the eastward drifting surface lows

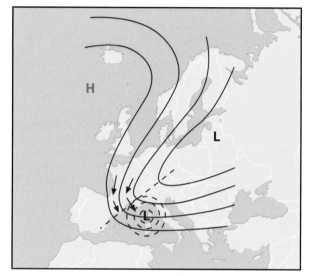

Figure 3.B.9 Onset of a Type 2 mistral: the upper level trough axis transits over the South coast of France, and NE to NW winds are found over SW France

With upper level features of Type (3), depressions are usually rapidly moving in an eastward direction through Europe, sometimes with a couple of day frequency. In this case mistral does not last long, but several episodes may follow one another. This is the typical case of drifting Atlantic depressions affecting most of central Europe, with pressure troughs extending into the south.

Evolution of upper level features is likely to develop like shown in Figure 3.B.10.

Initially, roughly two days before mistral onset, the upper level trough is usually located 10–20° of longitude west of the Iberian peninsula (T1). After about one day, the trough axis will likely have shifted east over western Spain (T2). Mistral will start when the 500hPa trough deepens over the south coast of France (T3) creating a strong northwesterly flow over western France, and to the west an upper level ridge builds at roughly the same longitude of Ireland and Spain.

Note that the trough may well be less pronounced than shown on the Figure: the most important factor is the presence of a NW flow over the bay of Biscay, with speeds of 50kn or greater. Any slight variations will slightly reduce the degree of confidence of the forecast.

At surface level depressions will likely follow the same path, drifting from the Atlantic ocean through the UK and France, then onto central Europe. *Figure 3.B.11*

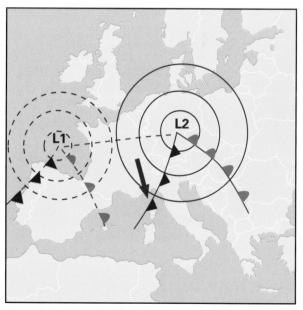

Figure 3.B.11 Usual surface low movement with a Type 3 mistral: various lows may follow one another, generating repeated mistral episodes

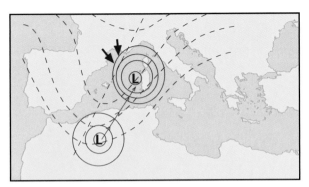

Figure 3.B.12 Another possibility of Type 3 mistral: an eastward drifting upper level trough causes a NWA low to approach the Gulf of Genoa/Corsica/Sardinia region

Another situation related to Type (3) mistral is depicted in Figure 3.B.12.

While the large scale upper level flow is still zonal, a transiting smaller scale upper level trough may extend from central Europe to north Africa, in which case a NWA depression may deepen, begin to drift towards the Gulf of Genoa and eventually generate mistral.

Mistral and Genoa depressions

Mistral is closely related to Genoa depressions. At its start, the cold air northerly flow meets the Alps and is channelled towards the southern coast of France; an area of low pressure begins to develop on the lee of the mountain range, and slowly deepens as mistral continues to blow. The circulation around the low increases and spreads mistral over a wide area, in turn mistral continues to help the low to deepen. The depression might eventually begin to migrate away from the Genoa region.

If mistral lasts sufficiently long, the accumulation of cold air north of the Alps will sooner or later be able to transit over the mountains, and cold northerly air will reach the Ligurian and northern Tyrrhenian Sea as Tramontana wind.

On average (Figure 3.B.13), as long as the centre of the low will remain inside the dashed square area, mistral is likely to blow/continue to blow. If the low drifts away, conditions for mistral existence will be weaker, and the wind might eventually stop blowing.

Additional Mistral forecasting aids

Mistral is most sensitive to pressure gradient along the coast of France. Rather than pressure tendencies at single points, it is often more useful to follow the barometric evolutions at all available coastal stations, in order to keep under control the evolution of the gradient in an east to west orientation.

If pressure values from coastal stations are available, mistral onset can be forecast when pressure difference between Perpignan and Marseille, or between Marseille and Nice reaches 3 hPa, or when between Perpignan and Nice the difference is 6hPa. This latitude-oriented pressure gradient generally occurs when the Genoa low is beginning to be more structured, and a closed low has appeared on surface charts.

Along the western side of French coast, the usual signs of a starting mistral are pressure rises, a stop in precipitations, skies getting clearer and dropping temperature; on the contrary, along the eastern side of French coast watch for a pressure drop, a stable or slightly rising temperature, the presence of rain and often some swell.

Direction and strength

Along the shore, mistral tends to follow the orientation of the valleys: it blows violently out of the Rhône valley from the north or northwest, it is more NW oriented in Provence, whereas more to the west, south of the Durance valley, its direction is more NNE. Locally, an already strong mistral may be increased by as much as 1–2Bft notches around Cap Béar and Cap Creus. In the middle of the Golfe du Lion its average direction is 320°–340°. To the east, it is westward oriented over south Corsica and Sardinia; whereas north of Corsica island it blows from a SW direction. *Figure 3.B.14*

Mistral often blows at gale to strong gale force, but cases of even stronger winds are not rare. In the open water on the Golfe du Lion winds in excess of 40kn occur about 10% of the time.

Pressure differences can be used to forecast typical wind strength in the Golfe du Lion.

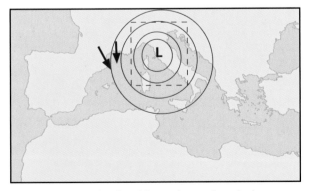

Figure 3.B.13 Mistral and Genoa lows: when the low centre drifts outside the boxed area, mistral usually abates

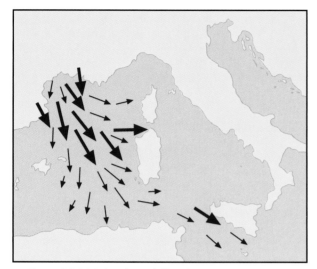

Figure 3.B.14 Mistral usual direction

Between Perpignan and Montpellier: 3hPa 8 Beaufort; 4hPa 9Bft; 5hPa 10Bft

Between Perpignan and Marseille: 5hPa 8Bft; 6/7hPa 9Bft; 9hPa 10Bft

Between Perpignan and Toulon: 7hPa 8Bft; 9hPa 9Bft; 10hPa 10Bft

Between Perpignan and Nice: 6/7hPa 7Bft; 8/9hPa 8Bft; 10hPa 9Bft; 12hPa 10Bft

Between Marseille and Nice: 4hPa 7/8Bft; 5hPa 9/10Bft

As the gradient between the stations at the two extremes (Perpignan and Nice) may not be homogeneous, it is important to collect as much information as possible about pressure at the intermediate stations: pressure reports from French signal stations ('Sémaphores') are quite useful as they cover much of the coast; they are usually broadcast at the end of VHF coastal bulletins.

Additional mistral strength determinants

The strongest speed usually occurs after the passage of the surface cold front, when the 500hPa trough transits over the Golfe du Lion.

Mistral speed over the open sea can be as much as double that measured at Perpignan or Marseille.

If surface isobars cross the valleys of Rhone or Garonne at 30°, the wind will likely be stronger.

If upper level 500hPa winds are above 65 knots over the Atlantic coast of France, mistral will exceed gale force and more likely reach storm force.

If a 500hPa area of lower temperatures can be identified on upper charts, to the west of a surface depression centred over the South of Italy, the strongest winds will likely be under it.

Area of influence

While mistral is usually a strong local wind of the South of France, its effects can sometimes be felt over a wide area. *Figure 3.B.15.*

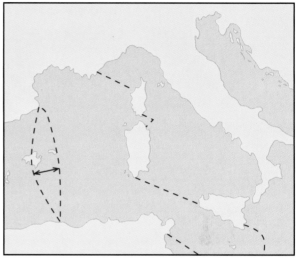

Figure 3.B.15 Usual extension of a widespread mistral

Southward, a widespread mistral can reach the northern shores of Africa, Sicily and even Malta islands. It is usually accelerated around the SW corner of Sardinia and then in the Sicily strait.

Laterally, wind speed is usually greatly reduced to the west by the Pyrenees, while to the east Corsica and Sardinia represent a natural barrier which is only occasionally passed by the wind, with the exception of the Strait of Bonifacio where mistral, of a westerly direction, is usually greatly accelerated.

To the east, mistral is likely to be limited to the area between the sheltering western edge of the Alps and Sanremo; it is rare along the western coast of Italy.

Figure 3.B.16 (overleaf) shows the likely mistral extension in case of a modest pressure gradient (a few hPa between Nice and Toulon); should this gradient increase to 5 or 6hPa then mistral is likely to extend a bit more towards Nice area.

To the west, the boundary covers a very narrow area (5–15 miles wide) usually located around a line passing through Perpignan, Mahon in the Balearic islands, and Bejaia in Algeria. The centre of this area can shift somewhat east or west from roughly SW Mallorca to NE Minorca. Winds to the west of the boundary may be as much as 3 or 4 Beaufort notches lower than those to the east; likewise, wave height can be three or four times lower. Around this

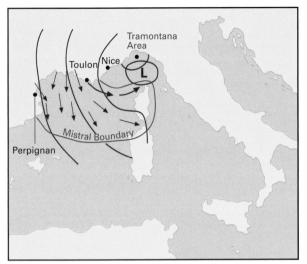

Figure 3.B.16 Area of mistral of limited extension

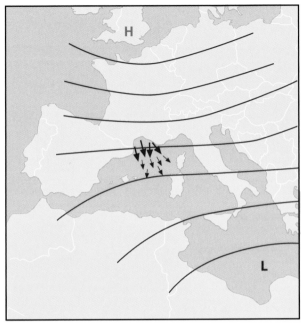

Figure 3.B.17 Typical Local mistral surface pressure distribution

boundary area, north of Mallorca, wind force during the day tends to be much stronger than at night, sometimes even double.

To the south and southeast, a strong mistral will extend as much as the 500hPa level trough does: it is not uncommon for it to reach the strait of Sicily and then Malta, or more seldom Algeria to the South.

Over the rim of mistral typical area, around Baleares, Corsica and Sardinia, mistral sometimes begins at night, with gusts becoming slowly stronger and more frequent.

When mistral distribution is more limited, it is often called Local Mistral. *Figure 3.B.17*

When a high pressure area is over France and the British islands (either a closed high or a ridge emanating from the Açores high), while a depression is located over the Ionian Sea, a NE flow can bring cold air from eastern Europe and generate mistral. Pressure gradient along the southern coast of France is usually limited, whereas a few hPa difference exists between central and southern France. In this case, mistral action is limited to the north of the Golfe du Lion, south of the Rhône valley and of the Camargue region, between Cap Creus or Cap Béar to the west, and Cap Sicié to the east. Wind force is still strong nonetheless.

Daily and seasonal variations

Mistral occurrences may happen all year long. The most violent cases usually occur during winter and spring. During late autumn and early winter, mistral may occur when water temperature is at least 6°C higher than air temperature.

Along the coast, wind strength peaks during the afternoon and it is lowest during the night, when temperature over land decreases and a layer of stable cold air slows the wind down. Its maximum speed in the afternoon is usually double its minimum speed during nighttimes.

Over the open sea on the contrary, daytime and night time speed variations are much reduced: average wind speed shows a minimum in the late afternoon, and a maximum only 3–5 knots higher early after midnight.

For these reasons, one must be careful before leaving port at night when mistral speed is lower, as away from the coast it may still blow at its usual strength.

Sea waves

Along the coast, the violence of mistral usually generates short, choppy seas with breaking waves. Like with any offshore wind, wave height increases farther from the coast, reaching an average of 5–6m. As with all wave systems, much higher waves are likely, 8–9m not being unheard of.

Cloudiness

Before the onset, cirrus clouds and fragmented altocumulus to the north or northwest are good signs of a likely mistral. Another sign of a likely mistral when the sky is cloudy and rainy, is the appearance of patches of blue sky to the west - northwest.

Once it has started, the sky is usually clear along the coast. The farther the cold air travels over the warm sea, the more likely convective clouds become.

During cases of extended mistral, a white band of clouds can develop in the area (usually to the NW of Sardinia) where the two main mistral axes converge: the NW one from SW France, and the NNE one from SE France; wind speeds are usually at their highest in this area.

Precipitation may or may not be present: two different kinds of mistral are usually defined.

White mistral

This is the most common type of mistral (it blows in Marseille sometimes more than 100 days a year. *Figure 3.B.18.*

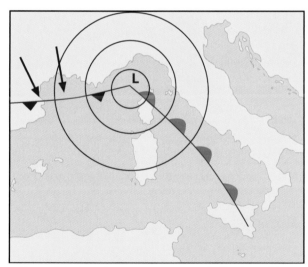

Figure 3.B.18 Surface pressure pattern indicating White mistral

A strong NW flow of cold air follows the passage of a front associated with a low pressure area over the Gulf of Genoa. A closed low is not strictly necessary, a 3hPa pressure gradient between Genoa and Perpignan can be enough to trigger the wind. Skies are clear, with very limited cloud cover; pressure suddenly rises with the passage of the front.

Black mistral

It develops when a low pressure over eastern Europe is associated to a high pressure ridge over the Iberian peninsula, and a succession of cold fronts transits from the NW over France. *Figure 3.B.19*

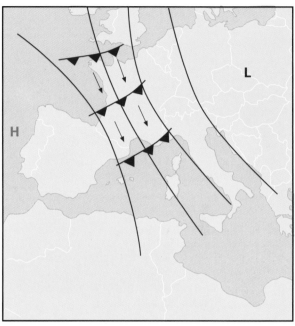

Figure 3.B.19 Surface pressure pattern indicating Black mistral

They bring a northwesterly inflow of moist, unstable polar maritime air which causes precipitations and cloudiness, often in the form of cumulonimbus with their associated gustiness. Pressure does not move much, and the wind usually does not decrease in strength between each front.

In both cases, visibility can be greatly reduced at sea level by the strength of the wind.

Cessation

In general, mistral will decrease or end whenever there is a reduction of the pressure gradient over southern France. This usually happens with either the filling of the Genoa low, or the weakening of the high pressure area over Spain or SW France.

In particular, wind speeds will decrease when a surface cyclonic circulation is replaced by an anticyclonic one, which is when surface winds veer N to NE.

1. Surface high pressure areas move into the western Mediterranean, while the Genoa low slowly fills or drifts eastward. *Figures 3.B.20 and 3.B.21.*

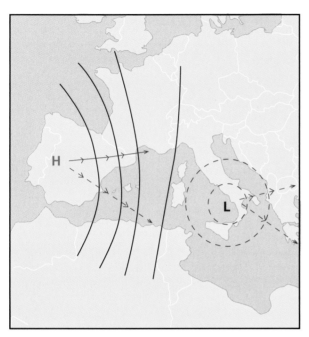

Figure 3.B.20 Mistral usually ends as high pressure from the west replaces an eastward drifting low pressure area

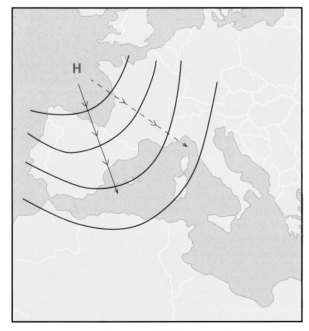

Figure 3.B.21 High pressure building over the central and western Mediterranean suggests an ending mistral

In this case the wind speed decreases locally and windy patches resist over the area. Once mistral has slowly ended, the weather will usually be fine.

2. The western high pressure surface ridge weakens. This may herald just a temporary cessation of mistral, as a new frontal system from the NW may follow and mistral conditions reappear after its passage.

3. The 500hPa ridge moves over the west central Mediterranean, or slowly weakens and disappears; or

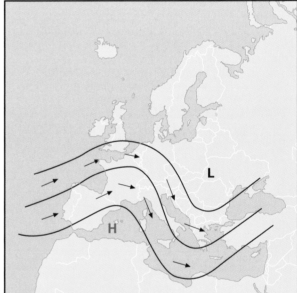

Figure 3.B.22 Mistral usually ends when an upper level ridge approaches western Europe

4. The upper level trough axis moves eastward, and is replaced by surface high pressure.

SIROCCO

The sirocco or scirocco is a wind blowing from north Africa into the Mediterranean from a SE to SW direction. It can affect almost any area of the Mediterranean basin, and depending on the region it may have slightly different characteristics, and is given several different names: Ghibli, Khamsin, Leveche, Chili, Simoon, Sharav, Marin, Autan, Largade, Yugo, etc.

It usually blows at its strongest in the Ionian Sea, especially in the southern part.

Sirocco can occur at any time of the year, although its frequency is higher during spring and autumn.

Being a desert wind, at its onset sirocco is very dry and dusty, although along its northward path, sirocco absorbs moisture from the sea and becomes very humid.

Formation and forecasting

Sirocco usually forms when pressure distribution causes desert air to be drawn northward into the southern Mediterranean.

This generally occurs with one of the following situations.

Type A a north Africa low drifting eastward will likely generate sirocco along its path, and especially over the Ionian Sea; sirocco will be more likely and possibly stronger if the low centre is located over the Gulf of Gabes. *Figure 3.C.1.*

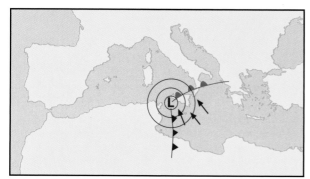

Figure 3.C.1 Type A sirocco is generated by NWA depressions

The path chosen by the low will dictate if sirocco will reach the Adriatic and Aegean Seas, or remain limited to the southern Mediterranean.

Type B a deep surface trough extending well into north Africa, whose axis is located between longitudes 10°E and 30°E. *Figure 3.C.2.*

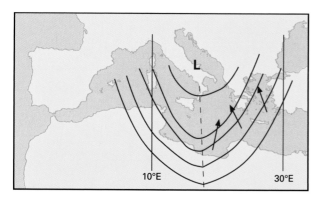

Figure 3.C.2 Type B sirocco is generated by a deep surface pressure trough

Type C typically, when a cold front crosses the Ionian or central Mediterranean, sirocco will usually be found in its eastern sector. *Figure 3.C.3.*

Figure 3.C.3 Type C sirocco is mainly generated by eastward drifting fronts

Type D a sirocco limited to the southern Ionian/ north African coast may be produced by a Sahara low whose centre is inland, and pushes an inverted trough of low pressure northward into the sea. *Figure 3.C.4.*

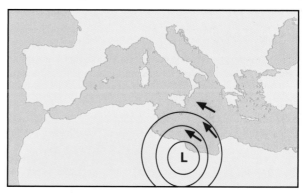

Figure 3.C.4 Type D sirocco: low pressure centred over North Africa

Additional forecasting aids

1. In general, sirocco will be associated to depressions crossing the Mediterranean. It will blow in their eastern side and have more or less marked features depending on the latitude of the depression. In particular when

2. A NWA low develops. *(See the relevant section.)*

3. If winds along southern Tunisian and Libyan coasts become southerly and their speed gradually increases, sirocco is then likely in the Ionian and eastern Mediterranean.

4. Sirocco is likely to blow at gale to strong gale force if 500hPa charts show: a) an upper level trough whose axis is west of a surface low, spreading south of latitude 30°N, and between longitudes 5°E and 25°E; and b) upper level wind speed over NWA of northwesterly direction, with speeds greater than 60kn. *Figure 3.C.5.*

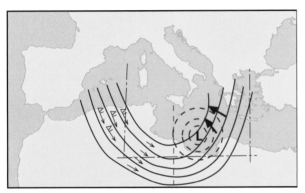

Figure 3.C.5 Strong sirocco generated by an upper level trough fuelling a surface low (dashed lines)

Direction and strength

Sirocco usually blows from a SE to SW direction. Isobars distribution will likely determine its direction over open sea areas like the Ionian Sea or the eastern Mediterranean, while orographic features like the Apennines will likely orient it from the southeast along the Gulf of Genoa, Tyrrhenian and Adriatic Sea. Channelling effects between Corsica and the Italian peninsula are likely to increase its strength by 1–2Bft notches, especially around Elba island.

Near the Middle East coast, sirocco usually blows from a more easterly direction.

When related to a deep developing NWA low, sirocco may commonly blow to gale or strong gale force in the Ionian Sea, especially around the Gulf of Gabes.

Sirocco can reach gale force and its direction be modified when orographic features increase air turbulence, and is sometimes signalled by middle level clouds showing a clear vertical development. This typically happens to the lee of mountainous islands. Around Sicily for example, along the northern and eastern shore the wind will be stronger and with more gusts then along the south; while seas will be lower on the north, overall weather conditions may be better along the southern coast.

Sirocco of storm force is rare.

Area of influence

Sirocco can blow all along the Mediterranean, from Gibraltar to the eastern edge of the sea. It occurs with a lower frequency over the western Mediterranean, while it is usually stronger and more likely eastward from Tunisia.

Seasonal variations

Sirocco winds can be found throughout all the year. As they are often associated with Sahara lows, their frequency is related and is maximum during spring and autumn.

During spring, sirocco is usually generated by situations of Type A.

During summer, sirocco is rare over the central and eastern Mediterranean, while it sometimes occurs over the western half.

During late autumn and winter sirocco is less likely on the western Mediterranean, as often an area of high pressure is located over north Africa, but can still blow from the Gulf of Gabes eastward.

Sea waves

As sirocco blows over wide open bodies of water with an extended fetch, and can last for a few days, high sea waves and considerable swell are common over the central and northern Mediterranean.

Cloudiness

Sirocco clouds and weather are greatly modified as it travels northward.

Along the African coast, sirocco is very dry and dusty, very hot during summer and warm during winter. Visibilities are usually bad, and can become dangerously low when sirocco blows to gale force and brings with itself large quantities of desert dust.

As it blows northwards over the open sea, sirocco gathers humidity: skies are overcast, low and middle level cloudiness increases, fog and light rain become quite common along the central and northern parts of the Mediterranean, especially if wind speed is limited. Once it dries, rain usually leaves a yellow/reddish dust deposit, a phenomenon which can occur even as far as northern Europe.

When sirocco comes in contact with orographic features, extensive fog and continuous drizzle usually occur.

Cessation

Sirocco will usually end when conditions for its development are no longer present.

In particular, the eastward movement of low pressure areas and related frontal passages usually mark the end of sirocco.

TRAMONTANA

Tramontana or tramontane is a term used in different locations of the western Mediterranean to generically indicate a cold northerly wind. Its Latin etymology means 'behind the mountains', as tramontana winds often blow downhill from mountain chains.

Over the Balearic islands and along the Spanish SE coast, tramontana is the generic name used for any northerly wind; it is indeed a trans-mountain wind as it blows downhill from the Pyrenees chain.

In the SW coast of France, 'tramontane' is often an alternative local name for mistral, although sometimes the underlying atmospheric phenomena may be slightly different.

Along the western Italian coast, tramontana is again a wind coming from 'behind the mountains', as it usually blows from N to NE over the northern Apennines into the Ligurian Sea, and over the central Apennines into the Tyrrhenian Sea.

The generating factors for tramontana are strictly related to those of mistral, gregale and bora, so a review of the descriptions of those winds may be useful.

There are four basic pressure patterns which are likely to generate tramontana.

Type A A high pressure area covers north central Europe, with a relatively lower pressure area over the Mediterranean creating a north to south gradient. This situation usually occurs during winter or early spring. Depending on different pressure distributions, tramontana may blow over the whole western Mediterranean or be limited to seas along the western Italian peninsula, from the Gulf of Genoa southward toward the Tyrrhenian. Figure 3.D.1.

Type B A strong and persistent north to northwesterly cold air flow, while generating mistral over the western Mediterranean will eventually cross the Alps and Apennines and generate a tramontana which will be limited to the Gulf of Genoa region. Like the former type, this situation is usually more likely during winter. Figure 3.D.2.

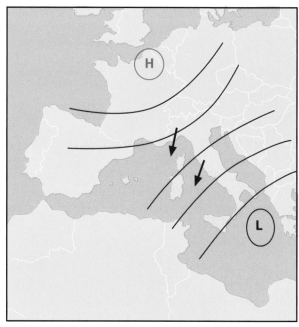

Figure 3.D.1 Type A tramontana is generated by a general north to south gradient over Western Europe

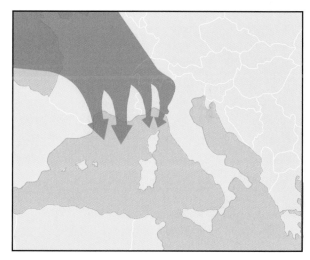

Figure 3.D.2 Type B tramontana is induced by northern cold air flow

Type C tramontana may develop as an evolution of mistral-generating pressure patterns. If the depression related with mistral is migrating eastward (be it a Genoa low moving east or southeastward, or a Balearic low directed towards central Europe), and a high pressure area is building from the UK to Spain, mistral will slowly be replaced by a slightly weaker tramontana over the sea facing southern France. The N to NE flow of cold continental air will also cross the Apennines and generate strong and gusty tramontana over the Gulf of Genoa region and the Tyrrhenian Sea. *Figure 3.D.3.*

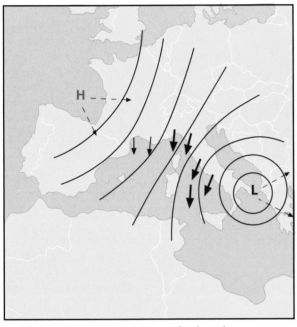

Figure 3.D.3 Type C tramontana slowly replaces a decaying mistral

Type D tramontana develops along the western coast of Italy following a strong bora outbreak in the Adriatic Sea (*see the relevant section for more details*). This is usually a winter situation. Cold continental air from the Balkans quickly flows across the Adriatic, crosses over the Apennines and when it reaches the Tyrrhenian Sea it shows a much increased gustiness, with an irregular distribution of wind speeds. Over the Tyrrhenian Sea, several areas may offer mild conditions, whereas at just a few miles distance tramontana may blow to gale force.

GREGALE

Gregale is the name given in several areas of the central Mediterranean to a strong, cold wind blowing from the NNE to ENE.

It is most frequent during winter, when it may climb to strong gale to storm force in the whole half of the Mediterranean west of the Aegean Sea meridian, in particular over the Ionian Sea.

Generally, a ridge from the Siberian high extends over central Europe, and generates a flow of cold continental air from the NE towards an area of low pressure over the Mediterranean; gregale is usually related to one of the different depressions which may affect the Mediterranean. *Figure 3.E.1.*

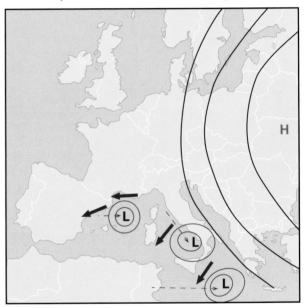

Figure 3.E.1 Gregale is usually associated with low pressure areas

When associated with an eastward drifting Balearic low, a strong gregale hits the SW coast of France and the whole SE coast of Spain. Its duration is usually a couple of days at most.

When associated to a Genoa low drifting southeastward, Gregale follows after mistral and Tramontana winds: isobars to the NW of the Genoa depression may remain packed and gregale blow fiercely over the Tyrrhenian Sea. Its duration is usually of a couple of days at most.

When associated with a NWA depression, gregale can be strong over the whole Ionian Sea, particularly around Malta island. In this case if the depression is moving slowly it may last up to four or five days.

LEVANTE

Levante is an easterly or northeasterly wind similar to gregale that occurs in an area from the SE coast of Spain to west of the Strait of Gibraltar.

Its name comes from the Latin Levare, which means to rise, levante coming from the direction of the rising sun.

It is usually moderate or fresh (not as strong as the gregale) in most areas, mild, very humid, associated with overcast and rainy skies.

It is most frequent from February to May and October to December, when it can blow to gale or strong gale creating high sea states along the Spanish coast, while during summer it is rare and weaker.

Levante generally occurs when there is a pressure gradient in the western Mediterranean from NW to SE (higher pressure to the north).

The flow is then subject to a channelling effect in the Alboran and Gibraltar areas, between the Iberian and Atlas mountains, which can locally modify pressure distribution. The result is very often an increase in wind speed in this sector, which can be felt in a narrow band (usually just a few miles wide, more seldom up to 20–30 miles) west of the Strait of Gibraltar.

Formation and forecasting

There are a few pressure patterns which can generate Levante.

Type A The most frequent pattern (especially during summer) is given by a ridge from the Açores high extending over the Iberian peninsula and SW France, while a lower pressure area (not necessarily a closed low) is present over north Africa. Levante tends to be stronger west of the Balearic islands and can blow up to strong gale over the Gibraltar Strait, while it may be non existent over Sardinia and Corsica. *Figure 3.F.1.*

Type B A wide high pressure ridge from northern Europe extends over central Europe, while a relatively low pressure area exists over the western Mediterranean, with the low centre west of Gibraltar. This pattern usually causes Levante winds in the whole western Mediterranean. If the pressure gradient is limited, levante effect along the western Mediterranean coast will likely be a limited increase in sea breezes strength. *Figure 3.F.2.*

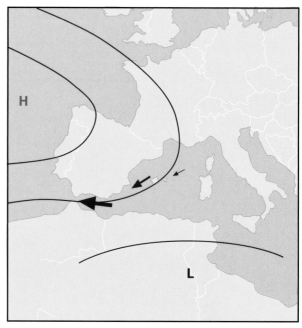

Figure 3.F.1 Surface pressure distribution leading to Type A levante

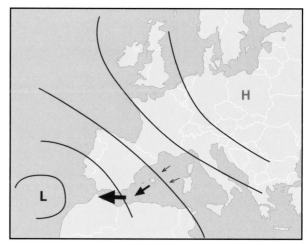

Figure 3.F.2 Surface pressure distribution of Type B levante

Type C If the high pressure area of pattern B. above is limited to the area around the Balearic islands, a local Levante will develop, limited to Alboran Sea area and Gibraltar strait. *Figure 3.F.3.*

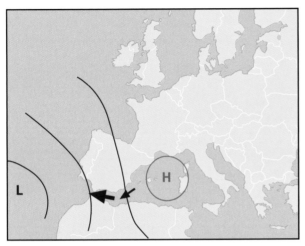

Figure 3.F.3 Surface pressure generating Type C levante, usually limited to the westernmost Mediterranean

Type D In association with a Balearic high pressure area, especially during late autumn and winter, Levante may blow before the passage of cold fronts coming from the Atlantic. *Figure 3.F.4.*

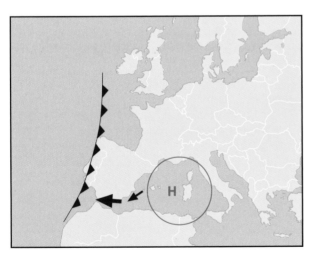

Figure 3.F.4 Levante associated with approaching Atlantic fronts

Type E A gale to strong gale or even more powerful Levante over the SE coast of Spain may be generated ahead of a deep low drifting eastward from Gibraltar. This is typically a winter situation, and the long fetch allows the wind to create very high sea states. *Figure 3.F.5.*

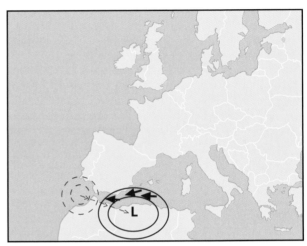

Figure 3.F.5 Levante associated with depressions drifting eastward over North Africa

On upper level charts, winds over the southern half of the Iberian peninsula from the NE and with speeds of 30kn or above are a very good sign that a strong levante is likely. *Figure 3.F.6.*

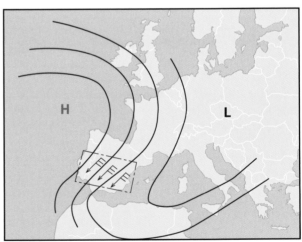

Figure 3.F.6 Example of 500hPa contours very likely to lead to levante: upper level winds over the boxed areas are from NE, with a speed in excess of 30kn

Additional forecasting aids

During summer, cold fronts transiting SW over Spain can cause the sudden appearance of Levante around Gibraltar and Alboran; if fronts are decaying, their passage can be detected by observing modifications of wind direction and humidity at coastal stations, especially Alicante and Malaga.

If a 300hPa constant pressure chart is available, upper level winds veering from the NW to the NE over the Iberian peninsula are a good indication of gale force Levante in the Gibraltar area.

West of Gibraltar, if low stratus clouds formations drift away from the coast of Portugal as far as 100–200 miles, then Levante is likely to develop later around Gibraltar.

Direction and strength

Levante direction usually shifts from the N–NE in the east of the western Mediterranean, to ENE to the west of the area, to east over Alboran and Gibraltar.

Levante usually reaches only 4/5 Beaufort in most of the western Mediterranean. Along the coasts, it usually combines with sea breezes, which tend to blow from a more easterly direction.

Over Alboran and the strait of Gibraltar, channelling effect may commonly increase Levante speed to gale or strong gale force.

Area of influence

During summer, Levante usually affects an area limited by the Algerian and Moroccan coasts, the Balearic islands, the western Mediterranean coast of Spain and the Atlantic immediately west of the Strait of Gibraltar.

Seasonal variations and cloudiness

Levante can occur throughout the whole year.

During summer, it is typically created by a pressure distribution of Type a., with the Açores high ridge reaching western Europe. Weather is usually fine, but fog or mist are frequent over Gibraltar and western Alboran regions (especially south of 36° latitude), as the wind comes in contact with colder waters.

During the rest of the year, Levante is mostly related to Balearic lows, NWA lows, or Atlantic depressions west of Gibraltar. Weather is usually cloudy and rainy, with heavy precipitations over the east coast of Spain. Cumulonimbus with gusts and thunderstorms may develop over the warm western Mediterranean waters if the flow coming from central Europe is made of sufficiently cold air.

Sea waves

While Levante does not usually create dangerous conditions, it can generate very high sea states in the Gibraltar area.

Cessation

a. Levante will usually end when surface troughs or fronts from Atlantic depressions cross over Spain, and bring along a generally western flow.

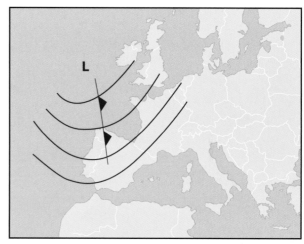

Figure 3.F.7 Levante usually ends when the surface trough axis transits over the Iberian peninsula

b. Levante is likely to end when the centre of a depression moves into (or develops in) the Alboran channel, east of Gibraltar. *Figure 3.F.8.*

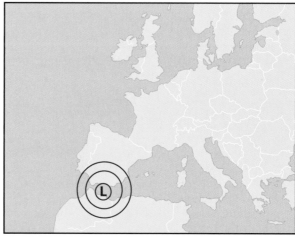

Figure 3.F.8 Levante cessation due to the presence of a low to the east of Gibraltar

4. Sea areas

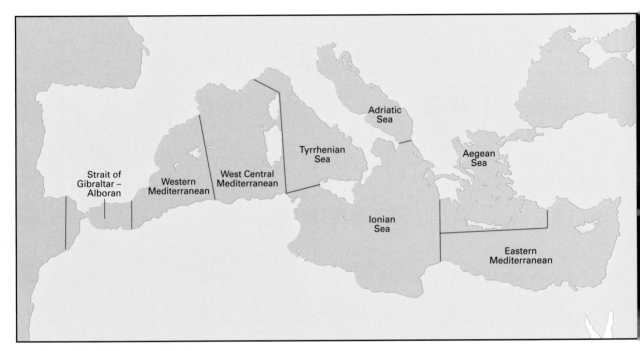

Figure 4.1 Mediterranean Sea Areas

The Mediterranean basin has been divided in eight sea areas, whose weather characteristics are more or less homogeneous.

The standard meteorological regions (as defined by the GMDSS system) included in each of these areas will be indicated in the text.

STRAIT OF GIBRALTAR – ALBORAN

1. Geographic features

This area extends from longitude 8°W on the Atlantic ocean side of the Strait, to 2°W, the longitude of Cabo de Gata on the Iberian peninsula. It roughly corresponds to GMDSS meteorological areas Cadiz, Strait of Gibraltar and Alboran.

High mountains to the north (Sierra Nevada) and to the south (western Atlas), together with the narrow sea strait between the European and African

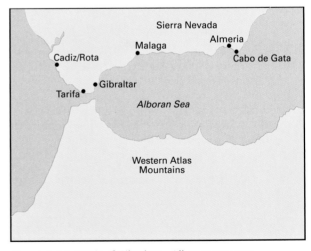

Figure 4.A.1 Strait of Gibraltar – Alboran sea area

continent accelerate the wind flow, and orient it in roughly an E–W direction.

Strong wind conditions in the Strait, coupled with tidal streams, often make for heavy and dangerous seas.

These effects are felt with less intensity over the western and eastern adjacent areas, which are more transition regions between the Strait and the western Mediterranean to the E, and the Atlantic Ocean to the W.

2. Seasonal weather overview

Winter

During winter, the Açores high usually drifts southward, and low pressure systems can freely cross the area, causing wet and windy weather, with mild temperatures. Westerly winds are more common than easterlies.

Easterly winds are rarer than during summer but they are stronger, usually blowing at 5–6Bft, but may reach higher speeds in the middle of the Strait. Low level cloudiness and reduced visibilities are usual features.

Westerly winds are equally strong, but usually show different characteristics. If from the NW they usually bring clear skies with only scattered showers and good visibility. If from the SW they usually bring heavy precipitations, gusts and thunderstorms; they are usually of shorter duration. Westerlies occur roughly 60% of the time.

During gale force episodes seas are usually high, and when the swell reaches the Strait the wave steepness increases, causing dangerous conditions for sailing.

Summer

During summer, the Açores high ridge extends over southwestern Europe and brings warm weather with prevalent light land-sea breezes over the area. Gales are rare. Calms roughly represent 10% of the observations. Easterlies are more frequent (roughly 60% of the time), although they usually show a reduced strength at 4–5Bft. They frequently generate fog or very low visibilities in the Strait.

Westerly winds are generally moderate from the NW and usually bring good weather.

Autumn

Autumn is a concentrated transition season: the month of October is usually the more chaotic, with an abrupt change from mild summer conditions to strong winter ones. Storm frequency is similar to winter.

Spring

Again, spring is transition season, with winter-like weather periods alternating with milder spells with summer features. Storm frequency is similar to winter.

3. Weather features and winds

Low pressure systems

Depressions affecting sailing conditions over the Strait of Gibraltar are usually of Atlantic or north African origin.

a. Atlantic lows to the west of the area usually follow one of the paths shown in Figure 4.A.2.

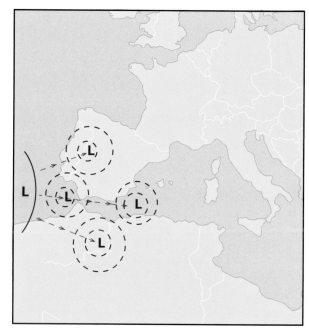

Figure 4.A.2 Usual paths of Atlantic depressions affecting the area

About one third of the depressions move eastward straight into Alboran (especially from autumn to spring) and usually generate gale force levante when sufficiently near to Gibraltar; a weakening of the lows to the west of Gibraltar is sometimes observed, but they may rapidly rebuild their strength once into the Mediterranean. (Incidentally, if during this kind of evolution 700hPa upper level winds back to 210° the low will likely transit through the Strait and levante conditions stop).

The other two thirds of depressions will either transit through the Iberian peninsula and develop westerly winds; or drift SE towards the south of the Atlas chain, where they merge or redevelop as NWA depressions,

b. NWA depressions: when located over Morocco or western Algeria they are usually responsible for levante wind over the Gibraltar/Alboran area.

See NWA and Levante section for a detailed description and forecasting.

c. A cut-off depression sometimes forms over the area: bad weather will be likely for a period of up to ten days, as these low usually remain stationary for several days.

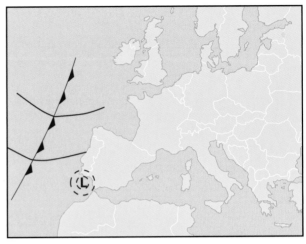

Figure 4.A.4 Local depression associated with an approaching Atlantic front

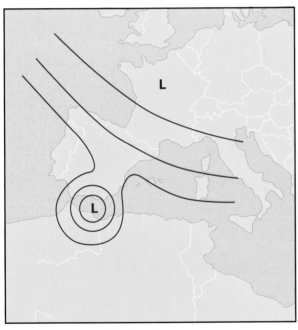

Figure 4.A.3 Cut-off surface low over the area

d. A local low pressure area may also develop immediately west of Gibraltar, in the Gulf of Cadiz, if a cold front roughly located between meridians 10°W and 30°W extends southward to 30°N–35°N. *Figure 4.A.4.*

Pressure features of lesser importance to sailing are:

a. The formation of an inverted low pressure trough (i.e. with lower pressure to the south) over the Iberian west coast. Northerly winds of force

4–5Bft usually develop along the Portuguese coast, whereas their speed will be lower over the western part of the Strait.

b. During late summer and early autumn, the inter tropical convergence zone sometimes drifts north, and short periods of bad weather can occur on the western side of the Strait before the disturbance drifts away.

Winds

Likely wind speeds at Gibraltar can be forecast through the pressure difference between coastal stations at Alicante and Casablanca. Gusts are usually 5–15 knots higher.

Pressure Difference	Easterlies	Westerlies
3–5hPa	10–15kn	10–15kn
5–10hPa	15–25kn	15–20kn
10–15hPa	25–30kn	20–30kn
Greater than 15hPa	30–40 kn	Greater than 30 kn

Wind strength associated with pressure difference between Alicante and Casablanca

Levante

See the relevant section for a description of levante characteristics and forecasting.

This wind is a major weather producer over the area.

Its likely strength in the area is rather well related to the pressure difference between Palma de Mallorca and Casablanca. A 6hPa difference usually creates a 5Bft levante, an 8hPa difference or more usually indicates 7Bft or above.

Similarly, in the Gibraltar strait pressure differences between Malaga and Cadiz can be used: 3hPa usually yields a 5Bft levante, 5hPa is indicative of gale force winds.

The likely wind speed in the Gibraltar strait is often the same as the one reported by Tarifa station.

A good indication of maximum wind speed in the strait is roughly given by the double of sustained wind speed at Gibraltar, although these conditions are usually limited to a few miles wide band in the middle of the strait, which may extend as much as 60 miles west of the Strait, north of 36° latitude.

Vendaval and Poniente

Vendaval and poniente are both westerly winds, which together with levante account for the great majority of wind occurrences over Gibraltar area.

Upper level 500hPa charts are often useful in predicting their behaviour.

Their onset is likely if either

a. A deep upper level trough extends over western Europe, and its axis roughly passes through the Strait.

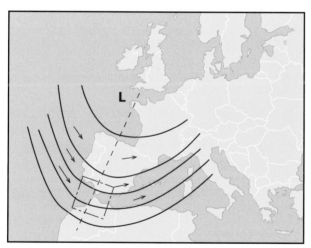

Figure 4.A.5 Westerlies generated by a wide upper level trough whose axis crosses the boxed area

b. Upper level contour lines are parallel, oriented west to east over the Strait, with upper air speeds of 50kn or above. *Figure 4.A.6.*

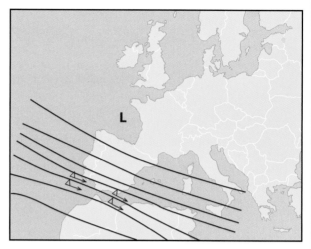

Figure 4.A.6 Westerlies associated with zonal flow with upper level wind speeds of 50kn or above

The likelihood of strong Westerlies will be slightly reduced if upper level features differ somewhat from those shown.

On surface charts, they can usually be generated by either a deep, wide low over the UK, or a depression transiting eastward over Spain, or a low pressure system over the western Mediterranean.

Westerlies are likely to end if either:

a. An upper level ridge arrives from the west over the area: this is sometimes announced one day in advance by the ridge axis around position T1, while westerlies would likely end when the axis has reached position T2. *Figure 4.A.7.*

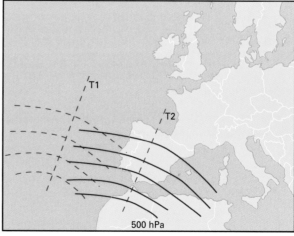

Figure 4.A.7 Westerlies cessation is likely when an upper level ridge axis reaches position T2

b. The maximum upper wind speed either significantly abates, or drifts south of the Atlas mountain chain.

Westerly winds in the Strait can usually be forecast to be gale to strong gale force if the pressure difference between Cadiz and Malaga is 4hPa or more. They will usually start when the upper level trough has moved east of the area.

Westerlies are usually stronger along the southern part of the channel.

If sailing from Gibraltar out of the Mediterranean, care should be taken as local wind speed may greatly underrate westerly force in the Strait.

Vendaval

It is a strong southwestern wind associated to low pressure systems transiting over central and southern Spain, generally occurring in the warm sector before the passage of a cold front over the area.

It is most likely during late autumn to early spring.

It usually blows to gale force, but in the Strait of Gibraltar it may be accelerated to storm force. Usually it does not last very long. Precipitation is heavy with violent gusts and thunderstorms, and usually starts several hours after the onset of the wind. Visibilities are reduced.

Poniente

It is a strong northwestern wind occurring after the passage of a cold front over the area.

Like the vendaval, it is most likely during late autumn to early spring, but can blow at any time of the year if high pressure builds to the west of Gibraltar.

An important phenomenon for navigation usually occurs on the Alboran Sea when a strong NW flow over the Iberian peninsula meets the southern Spain mountain chains (Sierra Nevada), Figure 4.A.8.: a lee trough develops along the northern coast of Alboran, causing weak W to SW winds near the shore, but 1–2Bft notches higher southwesterly winds along the north African coast to the south, which may well reach gale to strong gale force.

Skies are usually clear, visibilities excellent. Limited showers usually occur on the sea during the night.

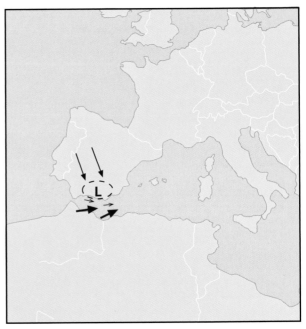

Figure 4.A.8 Surface lee trough developing to the south of Sierra Nevada mountains

Mistral

Mistral does not affect directly the area. However, it is worth noting that a strong mistral over the Golfe du Lion usually heralds gale force levante in the Strait, especially when a weak cold front drifts southwestward from the Golfe du Lion.

Southerly winds - Sirocco

See the relevant section for a description of sirocco characteristics and forecasting.

Over the Alboran Sea, a local southern wind named Leveche sometimes occur. Similarly to sirocco, it usually blows at moderate force though with gusts in the eastern sectors of a low, bringing hot and dusty wind over the area. It can often be forecast when a layer of brownish clouds appear to the south of the horizon.

Fog

Fog may occur at any time of the year, although it is more frequent from autumn through spring. It is usually denser in the early morning.

The worst episodes usually occur over Alboran, south of 36°N, often before the beginning of levante conditions (especially when levante follows after a long period of westerly winds).

4. Coastal weather bulletins

The Spanish coastal area to the west of Gibraltar is denominated 'Costa de Andalucia occidental y Ceuta'

The Spanish coastal area to the east of Gibraltar is denominated 'Costa de Andalucia oriental, Melilla y Alboran'

Algeciras Ch 74 0315, 0515, 0715, 1115, 1515, 1915, 2315 (in Spanish and English)

Almeria Ch 10, 67, 73 *Every odd hour +15mins (in Spanish and English)*

Cadiz Ch 26 *0940, 1140, 2140 (in Spanish)*

Cadiz Ch 74 *0315, 0715, 1115, 1515, 1915, 2315 (in Spanish and English)*

Cabo de Gata Ch 27 *0833, 1133, 2003 (in Spanish)*

Malaga Ch 26 *0833, 1133, 2003 (in Spanish)*

Tarifa Ch 81 *0833, 1133, 2003 (in Spanish)*

Tarifa Ch 10, 67, 73 *Every even hour +15mins (in Spanish and English)*

Gibraltar Radio FM 91.3–92.6–100.5MHz and AM 1458kHz *Every h+30mins usually from 0730 LT to 2030 LT*

Gibraltar BFBS FM 93.5–97.8MHz *Usually at 0745, 0845, 0945, 1202, 1602 LT (varies with day of the week)*

Ghazouet Ch 28 *0703, 2303 (English and French)*

Please note the area is also covered by several other services (Navtex, HF radio, Radiofax, etc): as most of them provide weather forecasts to several different areas, they have all been grouped at the end of the book.

See the Weather Forecast Appendix for more details.

WESTERN MEDITERRANEAN

1. Geographic features

This area extends from longitude 2°W, to a diagonal line from Cape St Sebastian on the Spanish coast (42°N 003°E) to the 5°E longitude area on the African coast. *Figure 4.B.1.*

It corresponds to meteorological areas Palos and Baleares, plus the western parts of areas Cabrera and Algeria.

To the north, it is limited by the Spanish southeastern coast, where mountain features (like the Sistema Ibérico and the Pyrenees chain) alternate with valleys (like Jucar and Ebro).

To the south, the African continent Atlas mountain chain extends throughout the area.

The eastern limit represents the mistral wind western boundary. *See Mistral section for more details.*

2. Seasonal weather overview

The weather behaviour over this area has many similarities with the one over Gibraltar–Alboran. *See the relevant section.*

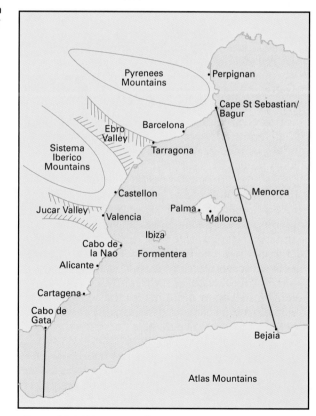

Figure 4.B.1 Western Mediterranean sea area

Summer

During summer, the area is usually under the influence of an Açores high ridge, which generates fine, dry weather. Winds are usually light (gale force occurs only 5% of the time), of easterly direction. Calms represent 5–6% of total observations.

Along the Spanish mainland coast, sea breezes usually increase to reach 4–5Bft in the early afternoon, and slowly end at sunset; night land breezes are usually weaker.

Along the northern coast of Mallorca, calms and light winds prevail, whereas along the south sea-breezes of easterly direction are common; winds veering to SW often announce the arrival of a depression. The southwestern Baleares like Ibiza and Formentera are under the direct influence of stronger easterlies which may last several days, any interruption in their flow usually foretells a change in weather.

Summer type weather usually lasts into early autumn, while in general during the month of October the weather changes rapidly into winter-like type.

Winter

During winter, the Açores high usually drifts south, leaving the door open to low pressure systems coming from the western quadrants. The weather is usually windy, with several gale or strong gale episodes (maximum yearly frequency), and precipitations abound. Winds are W to NW roughly 60% of the time.

Locally, along the northern coast of Mediterranean Spain, winds tend to blow from W, NW and SW; whereas along the southern coast they more frequently blow from SW.

The area around Minorca is under the direct influence of mistral and gregale winds, with a high frequency of gales (which are sometimes announced by a northerly to northeasterly swell). From late autumn to early spring seas are among the highest of the whole Mediterranean. The same kind of weather occurs along the N–NW coast of Mallorca island, albeit with lesser frequency, whereas its southern coast is more associated with westerly winds patterns. The southwestern Baleares (Ibiza, Formentera, etc) are decidedly under the influence of west to northwesterly winds.

During spring, weather alternate between winter-type and summer-type spells, until it settles to fine weather during the month of May. The months of March and April show a gale frequency higher than that of January and February.

3. Weather features and winds

Low pressure systems

Depressions affecting the area are usually related to one of the systems below.

a. Atlantic lows moving into the Mediterranean (mainly occurring from autumn to spring), usually generating gale force levante if sufficiently near to Gibraltar.

Roughly two thirds will either transit through the Iberian peninsula, or drift SE towards the south of the Atlas chain, where they will merge with or redevelop as NWA depressions. The other third will move through the Strait into Alboran and then possibly into the western Mediterranean. *See Figure 4.A.2. on Strait of Gibraltar – Alboran Section.*

b. NWA depressions. *See the relevant section for characteristics and forecasting.*

A particularly dangerous case of Sahara low evolution occurs when secondary lows develop on the sea north of the Atlas mountains. *(See Figure 4.B.2, dashed lines.)*

This is likely to happen when the upper flow over north Africa is from the SSW, or if a 500hPa closed low is visible over western Sahara (solid lines): these depressions may quickly deepen and cause very heavy weather over the area, although

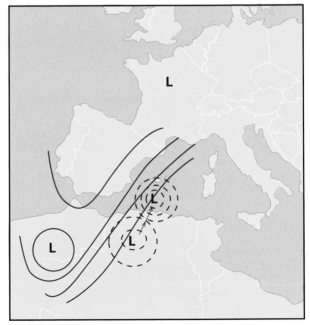

Figure 4.B.2 Upper level flow (solid lines) may bring a deepening NWA depression into the area

they usually do not last long. Among the most severe storms of the area there are a few cases when a low from NWA merged with a low pressure coming from the bay of Biscay or the Balearics, and meteorological 'bombs' developed.

c. Balearic Sea depressions. *See the relevant section for characteristics and forecasting.*

These lows may develop winds to strong gale or storm force, especially when a cold front crosses Spain eastward. These fronts should be followed closely, as they sometimes seem to slow down or disappear altogether when on land but re-generate once over the Mediterranean.

Seas are usually heavy and confused after the frontal passage.

Gregale

See the relevant section for characteristics and forecasting.

Gregale can be particularly strong (up to strong gale force, as far south as Ibiza island) when a drifting low enters the area from Alboran or southern Spain.

Levante

See the relevant section for characteristics and forecasting.

In the area, levante is more likely during autumn and spring, and it happens more frequently than over the Alboran area.

It is usually associated with heavy precipitations and heavy seas.

Vendaval and Poniente

See the Westerly wind section under the Gibraltar zone chapter for characteristics and forecasting.

Vendaval is a strong SW wind affecting in particular the southern portion of the area, especially during late autumn and early spring. It sometimes reaches gale force, but usually does not last long. Vendaval common occurrence is before a frontal passage.

Poniente, named Cierzo along the Ebro valley, comes more from the NW. It usually occurs when a sufficient pressure gradient exists from NW to SE Spain, or commonly after the passage of a front from Spanish mainland to the SE.

Wind speed tends to follow the pattern shown in Figure 4.B.3.

Along the coast, the wind is weaker around Barcelona, increases becoming gusty at the mouth of the Ebro river, then drops by 1–3Bft notches and

Figure 4.B.3 Typical Cierzo speed and directions

tends to back to W or SW. If the NW flow is well established, another area of stronger NW winds may be found near the Valencia area.

As one travels away from the coast, nearer to the Balearic islands, variations in wind speed tend to even out, and a strong NW is usually found everywhere over the area.

At Valencia and in front of the Ebro valley wind speeds are usually highest in the morning or early afternoon, while they usually slow down during the evening.

Mistral

Mistral main area of influence is east of the area under discussion, which will be examined in next chapter.

Its occurrence in the western Mediterranean is limited to around the eastern boundary of the area. (*See under 1. Geographic features, page 44.*)

As mistral western boundary may oscillate E–W, from western Mallorca to eastern Minorca, mistral conditions are likely to be limited to this sector. To the west of this line going from Perpignan over Minorca island, then to Bejaia on the Algerian coast, conditions are likely to be fine, whereas to the east mistral is likely to blow at its full strength.

If mistral hits while sailing near the boundary, the safest course will be westward, possibly looking for additional shelter on the lee of Balearic islands.

See the relevant section for characteristics of mistral western boundary and forecasting.

Sirocco

See the relevant section for characteristics and forecasting.

In the western Mediterranean sirocco is most frequent during April, May and June. Although it can be gusty, its speed is usually moderate, and seldom reaches gale force.

Visibilities are usually reduced everywhere: along the north African coast because of desert dust, along the northern part of the area because of low level clouds created by moisture picked up by the wind over the sea.

Fog

Fog is most likely all along the north African coast, especially during summer.

Reduced visibilities along the Spanish coast are usually due to sirocco conditions, whereas around the Balearic islands they are usually caused by low level clouds and precipitations occurring mainly during winter and spring.

4. Coastal weather bulletins

VHF (All times UTC)
The Spanish coastal area is divided into 'Costa oriental de Andalucia, Melilla Y Alboran' (for a small segment immediately north of Cabo de Gata), 'Costa de Murcia y la Comunidad Valenciana', 'Costa de Cataluña' and 'Costa de la Illes Baleares'.

Alicante Ch 85 *0910, 1410, 2110 (in Spanish)*

Bagur Ch 23 *0910, 1410, 2110 (in Spanish)*

Barcelona Ch 60 *0910, 1410, 2110 (in Spanish)*

Barcelona Ch 10 *0600, 0900, 1500, 2000 (winter)*
0500, 0900, 1400, 1900 (summer) (in Spanish and English)

Cabo de Gata Ch 27 *0833, 1133, 2003 (in Spanish)*

Cabo de la Nao Ch 01, 02 *0910, 1410, 2110 (in Spanish)*

Cartagena Ch 04 *0910, 1410, 2110 (in Spanish)*

Cartagena Ch 10 *0115, 0515, 0915, 1315, 1715, 2115 (in Spanish and English)*

Castellon Ch 25 *0910, 1410, 2110 (in Spanish)*

Castellon Ch 74 *0903, 1403, 1903 (in Spanish and English)*

Ibiza Ch 03 *0910, 1410, 2110 (in Spanish)*

Menorca Ch 85 *0910, 1410, 2110 (in Spanish)*

Palamos Ch 13 *0630, 0930, 1330, 1830 (in Spanish and English)*

Palma de Mallorca Ch 10 *0735, 1035, 1535, 2035 (winter)*
0635, 0935, 1435, 1935 (summer) (in Spanish and English)

Palma de Mallorca Ch 20 *0910, 1410, 2110 (in Spanish)*

Tarragona Ch 23 *0910, 1410, 2110 (in Spanish)*

Tarragona Ch 74 *0530, 0930, 1530, 2030 (winter)*
0430, 0830, 1430, 1930 (summer) (in Spanish and English)

Valencia Ch 10, 67 *Every even hour +15mins (in Spanish and English)*

Alger Ch 84 *0733, 2333 (English and French)*

Annaba Ch 24 *0703, 2303 (English and French)*

Arzew Ch 27 *0703, 2303 (English and French)*

Bejaia Ch 26 *0733, 2333 (English and French)*

Ghazouet Ch 28 *0703, 2303 (English and French)*

Oran Ch 25 *0703, 2303 (English and French)*

Skikda Ch 25 *0703, 2303 (English and French)*

Tenes Ch 24 *0733, 2333 (English and French)*

Please note the area is also covered by several other services (Navtex, HF radio, Radiofax, etc): as most of them provide weather forecasts to several different areas, they have all been grouped at the end of the book.

See the Weather Forecast Appendix for more details.

WEST CENTRAL MEDITERRANEAN – GOLFE DU LION

1. Geographic features

This area is limited to the west by a line going from cape St Sebastian on the Spanish coast, to Bejaia on the Algerian coast; its eastern boundary is roughly the meridian running along the eastern coasts of Corsica and Sardinia; and from the north tip of Corsica to the French / Italian border on the coast. Figure 4.C.1.

It covers the following GMDSS meteorological standard areas: Lion, Minorca, the eastern parts of Cabrera and Algeria, Provence, Corse, Bonifacio, Sardinia, Annaba and the western part of zone Tunisia.

To the north, the mountain range of the complex Pyrenees – Massif Central – Alps presents two major openings at the Toulouse/Carcassonne gap and at the river Rhone Valley.

To the east, Corsica and Sardinia, two major Mediterranean islands represent a boundary from the different weather area of the Tyrrhenian Sea.

To the south, the Atlas mountains run almost uninterruptedly along the African coast.

The western limit is represented by the weather boundary of mistral wind (*see the relevant section*).

2. Seasonal weather overview

Winter

The Açores high having drifted south, the area is under the repeated influence of outbreaks of cold northerly air, and the passage/development of low pressure systems. These are responsible for extended periods of bad weather with winds from gale to violent storm force.

Mistral accounts for the majority of such events, and may occur as much as 20% of the time, especially in the northern half of the area.

Along the eastern portion of the South coast of France, long periods of calms are interrupted by easterly and southwesterly gale episodes (gregale and libeccio), or mistral tails which here tends to be oriented W–WSW.

The northern coast of Africa has a lower frequency of gales, roughly one third that of the north. Prevailing winds usually blow W to NW and can raise heavy seas along the coast, and although mistral does not reach the north Africa coast too often, its swell often does. Southwesterly gales occur along the western part of the coast when a secondary low pressure area develops south of the

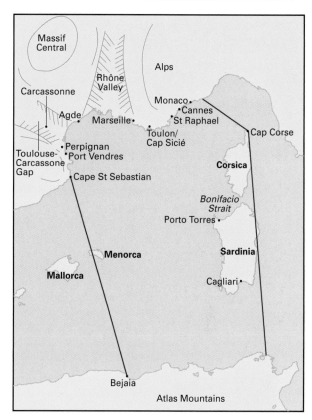

Figure 4.C.1 West central Mediterranean – Golfe du Lion sea area

Iberian peninsula. Thunderstorms are not rare along the eastern part of the north African coast.

Other bad weather occurrences are caused by low pressure systems and associated frontal features (Atlantic lows, Balearic lows, Genoa lows, etc).

Summer

An Açores high ridge usually extends northeast towards central Europe, and pushes more to the north the average path of depressions. The weather is usually nice and warm, sea-land breeze winds are the norm. Although rarer than during winter, mistral often makes its appearance, especially over the Golfe du Lion area.

Spring and autumn

They usually show a succession of periods of winter and summer-type weather, until one of the two prevails.

During spring, this transition lasts slightly longer, usually taking two or three months before mistral events get rarer and summer weather settles in.

Autumn on the other hand is usually limited to the month of October, with summer weather usually lasting until the end of September, and well established winter-type phenomena from November onward.

3. Weather features and winds

Low pressure systems

Depressions having an influence over the area are generally of three different types.

1. Balearic depressions. *See the relevant section for characteristics and forecasting.*

    These pressure systems have the greatest influence over the area. They have two main paths: either they drift N–NE towards the south coast of France, or they move to the SE across the open sea; in both cases, if they deepen sufficiently they create strong winds and heavy seas in all the area. Winds are oriented around the low pressure centre in the typical manner, usually with southwesterlies to the south, and winds from NE to SE to the north of the low centre.

2. NWA lows. *See the relevant section for characteristics and forecasting.*

    The main effect of these lows is sirocco (*see below*), which along the north African coast may blow E to SE to gale or strong gale force.

    An important, though rare, heavy weather producer for the area is the development of a secondary low over the sea, north of the Atlas mountains, at the same time as a NWA depression develops on land. These lows can bring E to NE gale to violent storm conditions with thunderstorms along the coast, but usually do not last long.

    They often form with an upper level flow from the S to SW over the Atlas mountains, and usually drift east in parallel with the dominant low over land. If the upper level flow backs to the SE though, they may remain stationary; if they come in contact with a frontal area they may deepen quite rapidly and become a major independent depression.

3. The Genoa lows. *See the relevant section for characteristics and forecasting.*

    The main influence of Genoa depressions is related to mistral: when the Genoa low is well developed, mistral conditions tend to be stronger and affect a wider area. *See the Mistral section for more details.*

At times, two or three of these different types of lows coexist at their early development stage. A wide area of low pressure but with very weak gradients may extend over the whole western Mediterranean, sometimes accompanied by frontal areas with weather features like isolated showers and thunderstorms.

In this case, some help about the likely evolution may be found in upper level charts. Whenever a 500 hPa trough approaches a weak surface low, this is more likely to develop into a more organized depression, which usually follows one of the typical evolutions described in the relevant sections.

Mistral

See the relevant section for characteristics and forecasting.

Mistral is by far the greatest concern for sailors in this area at any time of the year.

Over the NE part of the area, between the south coast of France and Corsica, mistral roughly blows to gale force one tenth of the time during the period from late autumn to early spring, while it is less likely during summer. Often, mistral over Corsica is of the black type, even if nearer the continent it is of white type.

Sometimes along the SE coast of France/NW coast of Italy, a small scale cyclonic circulation develops on the lee of the mountains, Figure 4.C.2, and NW to W winds near Toulon/Cap Sicié are often opposed to NE to E winds blowing from the Italian side.

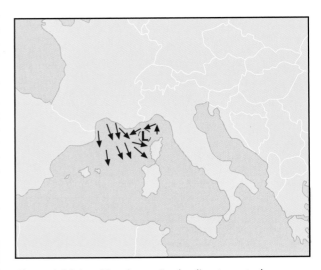

Figure 4.C.2 Local lee depression leading to easterly winds along SE France/NW Italian coasts

A strong channelling effect occurs on the Bonifacio strait, between Sardinia and Corsica: here mistral may blow with a westerly direction with speeds often in the range of 8/9Bft with gusts, creating high seas. It often extends several miles east of the Strait.

To the south, the coast of Africa is sometimes under the effect of a widespread mistral, especially with a well developed Genoa depression: conditions tend to worsen approaching the eastern third of the area, near the strait of Sicily: waves of 4–6m and winds in the 8/9Bft range are not uncommon, especially during winter.

Its western boundary is usually well represented by a line from Perpignan to Bejaia in the Algerian coast, whose middle part crosses the Balearic archipelago somewhere between SW Mallorca and NW Minorca. While sailing in this area, shelter can usually be found on the lee of these islands, or by keeping a westward course.

Gregale

See the relevant section for characteristics and forecasting.

Over the central and southern parts of the area, gale force gregale is usually associated to sufficiently developed NWA depressions.

Over the northern part of the area, gregale is more related to Balearic depressions or Atlantic depressions drifting southeastward from the Gulf of Biscay. East of Toulon (where gregale is generally related to deep Genoa lows) it is likely to be E to NE, whereas to the west in the Golfe du Lion it tends to be southeasterly. Around Corsica, the wind is greatly accelerated at Bonifacio strait and around the northwestern coast, while a relative shelter can be found along the southwestern coast.

On both cases, a rapid building of a high pressure area over northern Italy may contribute to greatly increase wind strength.

Sirocco

See the relevant section for characteristics and forecasting.

Gale episodes occur a few times a month during the transition seasons.

Along the northern coast of Africa, it is mostly moderate though gusty. It is usually dry but desert dust can greatly affect visibilities.

Along the southern coast of France sirocco is usually named Marin, and its direction may vary locally from SW to SE (when it usually takes the name of Autan).

In some cases, sirocco over the open sea may be associated with Local Mistral along the coast. (*See Local mistral under the relevant section for more details.*)

During all sirocco occurrences in the northern half of the area, low level clouds, light rains and sometimes fog will be likely.

Libeccio

Gale force SW winds are frequently associated with Genoa cyclogenesis, especially in the sea area from southern France to Corsica.

Libeccio may cause heavy seas along the western coasts of Corsica and Sardinia, and usually brings bad weather and precipitations.

Tramontana

See the relevant section for characteristics and forecasting.

Tramontana can blow to gale to strong gale force around Cap Corse, on the northern tip of Corsica island.

Winds around Corsica and Sardinia

To the north, NW to SW winds are prevalent all year long, more so during summers. They are usually strongly accelerated around the northern tip of Corsica.

The eastern Corsican and Sardinian coasts are more sheltered from westerlies, which are a concern to navigation usually at the mouth of the few valleys along the mountain range. Libeccio often blows with gusts, accelerated by foehn effects. Gales from the N to NE are not uncommon during winter.

The Bonifacio strait with Sardinia usually strongly accelerates the prevalent easterly or westerly winds.

Along the western coasts breezes are the prevalent summer phenomenon, usually blowing not stronger than 4–5Bft. Gales are generally from WNW to SW, and more frequent during winter. Cirrus clouds often precede mistral onset by 12–24 hours.

The southern third of Sardinia is where sirocco is of some importance, especially during early spring; other gale force episodes are usually caused by gregale winds.

Useful signs of approaching bad weather are the absence of sea breezes around the two islands during summer, oncoming swells from the open sea while winds are still light, and the rise of the sea level inside port areas.

Fog

Areas where fog is most likely include the Golfe du Lion, the coast around Corsica and Sardinia and the sea stretch between Sardinia and Tunisia.

Along the African coast, visibilities can be greatly reduced by sand and dust storms, which are usually short lived though.

4. Coastal weather bulletins

VHF

All coastal weather bulletins are broadcast after a general call on channel 16.

SPANISH BORDER TO PORT CAMARGUE

Port Vendres Ch 79 *0703, 1233, 1903 local time*

Agde Ch 79 *0715, 1245, 1915 local time*

PORT CAMARGUE TO SAINT RAPHAEL

Planier Ch 80 *0733, 1303, 1933 local time*

Toulon Ch 80 *0745, 1315, 1945 local time*

Cannes Ch 80 *0746, 1316, 1946 local time*

Monaco Radio Ch 25 *Continuous (three daily updates), in English and French*

SAINT RAPHAEL TO MENTON

Cannes Ch 80 *0803, 1333, 2003 local time*

Monaco Radio Ch 23 *Continuous (three daily updates), in English and French*

French bulletins often report pressure and wind conditions at the following coastal signal stations, which can be helpful in checking mistral conditions.

Bear–Port Vendres, Leucate, Sète, Espiguette–Le Grau du roi, La Couronne–Martigues, Bec de l'Aigle–La Ciotat, Cepet– St Mandrier, Porquerolles, Camarat–Ramatuelle, Cap Dramont–St Raphael, La Garoupe–Antibes, Cap Ferrat–St Jean Cap Ferrat.

French Signal Stations

Corsican Signal Stations

CORSICA ISLAND

Ersa Ch 79 *0733, 1233, 1933 local time*

Serra di Pigno Ch 79 *0745, 1245, 1945 local time*

Conca Ch 79 *0803, 1303, 2003 local time*

Serragia Ch 79 *0815, 1315, 2015 local time*

Punta Ch 79 *0833, 1333, 2033 local time*

Piana Ch 79 *0845, 1345, 2045 local time*

Monaco Radio Ch 24 *Continuous (three daily updates), in English and French*

French bulletins often report pressure and wind conditions at the following coastal station around Corsica island. *See Figure above for their locations.*

Pertusato–Bonifacio, Chiappa–Porto Vecchio, Alistro, Cap Sagro, Cap Corse, Ile Rousse, Ajaccio–La Parata.

An interesting lexical detail, especially in Mistral prone areas, is the conventional meaning of 'Rafales' (Gusts) in Meteo France bulletins.
'Rafales' means gusts 10–15kn above average wind speed
'Fortes rafales' means gusts 15–25kn above average wind
'Violentes rafales' means gusts more than 25kn above average wind speed

Italian 'Meteomar' weather bulletin

Ch 68 *Continuous (in English and Italian) (All areas)*

Meteomar bulletins can also be received from the following local emitters (their range varies, so it is advisable to try and listen to the various channels to detect which station provides local coverage):

P. Campu Spina Ch 82 *0135, 0735, 1335, 1935 (Sardinian Sea, Sardinian channel, Central and Southern Tyrrhenian)*

Margine Rosso Ch 62 *0135, 0735, 1335, 1935 (Sardinian Sea, Sardinian channel, Central and Southern Tyrrhenian)*

Monte Serpeddi Ch 04 *0135, 0735, 1335, 1935 (Sardinian*

Sea, Sardinian channel, Central and Southern Tyrrhenian)

Porto Cervo Ch 26 *0135, 0735, 1335, 1935 (Corsican Sea, Sardinian Sea, Central Tyrrhenian)*

Monte Moro Ch 28 *0135, 0735, 1335, 1935 (Corsican Sea, Sardinian Sea, Central Tyrrhenian)*

Osilo Ch 26 *0135, 0735, 1335, 1935 (Corsican Sea, Sardinian Sea, Central Tyrrhenian)*

Cagliari Ch 25, 27 *0135, 0735, 1335, 1935 (Sardinian Sea, Sardinian channel, Central and Southern Tyrrhenian)*

Monte Limbara Ch 85 *0135, 0735, 1335, 1935 (Corsican Sea, Sardinian Sea, Central Tyrrhenian)*

It should be noted that Meteomar is technically an offshore bulletin as it is related to wide sea areas, but the same text is also used for coastal forecasts. When sailing in areas where coastal features have a relevant impact on wind characteristics, it is advisable to keep in mind that the bulletin may not consider many of these local modifications, hence adjust accordingly the forecast contents.

Monaco Radio Ch 20 and Ch 22 *0930, 1403, 1930 Local time; Gale warnings at H+03 – (NW Mediterranean offshore areas)*

Menorca Ch 85 *0910, 1410, 2110*

Please note the area is also covered by several other services (Navtex, HF radio, Radiofax, etc): as most of them provide weather forecasts to several different areas, they have all been grouped at the end of the book.

See the Weather Forecast Appendix for more details.

TYRRHENIAN SEA

1. Geographic features

The Tyrrhenian area is limited to the NE by the coast of the Italian peninsula, to the south by the northern coast of Sicily then to the northeastern tip of Tunisia. From there, northward to Cap Corse, then to the French/Italian border on the coast.

It includes GMDSS meteorological areas Ligure, Elba, Maddalena, Lipari, Carbonara and the eastern Tunisia area. (Denominations in use in the Italian Meteomar weather bulletins are Mar Ligure and Mar Tirreno – northern, central, southern, eastern and western).

The Alps to the north, the Apennines to the east, the three big islands Corsica Sardinia and Sicily, there are many elements having a definite influence over local weather.

Channelling effects over Bonifacio strait (between Corsica and Sardinia), Messina strait (between Sicily and the Italian peninsula), Corsica strait (between Corsica and Elba island) and Sicily strait (between Sicily and Tunisia) are worth remembering, as with sustained winds these areas usually show a marked deterioration of weather conditions.

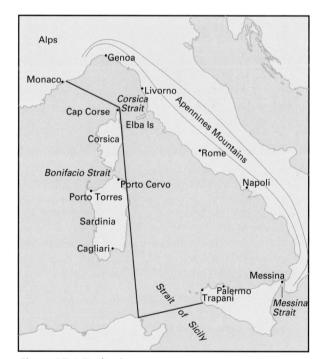

Figure 4.D.1 Tyrrhenian sea area

2. Seasonal weather overview

The most important weather producers in the area are Genoa depressions. Although they may form at any season, their intensity is somewhat different during the cold or the warm season.

Winter

During winter, the Açores high usually drifts south over the Atlantic ocean, giving free room for westerly flows over the area. Depressions develop in the Genoa Gulf area, and weather over the area is usually unsettled and often windy, with N–NE and SW winds accompanying the lows.

Gales and heavy seas are occasional, and can occur until early spring. They are relatively rarer in the southeastern Tyrrhenian, where southerly winds show a higher frequency than to the north of the area.

NW and SE gales often occur in the channels between Sicily and Sardinia and Tunisia.

Summer

The Açores high ridge northward migration pushes the westerly flow to the north of Europe: fine, dry weather with light breeze is usually found throughout the area, sometimes coupled with low visibilities.

Calm wind frequency is among the highest in the whole Mediterranean, especially over the southern half of the area.

Genoa depressions formation may occasionally deteriorate conditions for short periods of time.

Autumn and Spring

As it occurs in other areas, central Mediterranean autumn usually lasts just the month of October, with a rather abrupt transition from a summer-like weather to a winter type.

Again, spring characteristics are similar, although the transition from winter weather to summer weather usually takes a few months of alternating weather of different type.

It is worth noting the high frequency of thunderstorms along the SW coast of the Italian boot (sometimes accompanied by waterspouts).

3. Weather features and winds

Low pressure systems

1. Genoa depressions. *See the relevant section for characteristics and forecasting.* They are the main weather producing feature of the area.

2. NWA depressions. *See the relevant section for characteristics and forecasting.* These lows usually affect only the southern portion of the area. When they create southeasterly winds over the area, precipitation is not uncommon, and later a more defined warm front may develop over the central and south Tyrrhenian.

Mistral

See the relevant section for characteristics and forecasting.

The northern part of the area is very rarely affected by mistral, except at the northern tip of Corsica.

Sometimes along the SE coast of France/Ligurian coast of Italy, a small scale cyclonic circulation develops on the lee of the mountains, Figure 4.C.2., and NW to W winds near Toulon and Cap Sicié are often opposed to NE to E winds blowing from the Italian side.

Mistral may occasionally reach the central Tyrrhenian, where its direction is usually shifted to the SW.

A strong mistral can also be experienced for several miles eastward of the Bonifacio strait.

It is not uncommon in the southwestern region, south of Sardinia and to the NW of Sicily. This usually occurs when an upper level trough extends

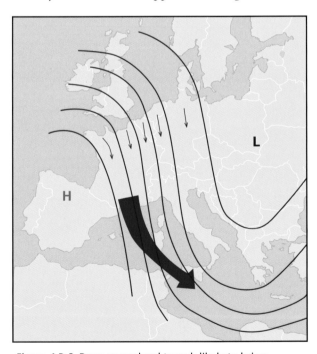

Figure 4.D.2 Deep upper level trough likely to bring mistral to south Sardinia and western Sicily

south from central Europe, and a region of NW upper flow reaches the south of Sardinia.

Tramontana

See the relevant section for characteristics and forecasting.

Tramontana may blow with gale force all along the Italian coast, from the Genoa Gulf to northern and central Tyrrhenian.

Sirocco

See the relevant section for characteristics and forecasting.

As usual, sirocco is generally associated to the warm sector of depressions transiting over the area.

Over the Gulf of Genoa, it usually blows from the S or SE, it usually generates a heavy swell, and visibilities can be reduced by low level clouds and precipitations. Sometimes, local northeasterly breezes may affect an area extending several miles from the coast, but sirocco conditions be experienced over the open sea.

Over the northern and central Tyrrhenian, when the wind blows from the SE light precipitations, fog and low level clouds may considerably reduce visibilities, especially along the eastern coast of Sardinia. These effects are less important over the southern Tyrrhenian, as air is relatively less humid.

Over the Sicily strait, gale force sirocco can raise heavy, breaking seas.

Along the northern coast of Sicily, sirocco is usually modified by a foehn effect, with dry, gusty winds with very limited precipitations.

Libeccio

Winds from the S or SW are generally caused by drifting depressions (*see above*). They generally cause heavy swells along the entire Italian coast, especially during the winter season.

Fog

Fog (and reduced visibilities) is usually associated with sirocco weather, especially in the area between Sardinia, Sicily and Tunisia, when it generally lasts one or two days.

Other areas prone to fog formations are the coasts of Corsica, Sardinia and northern Tyrrhenian.

Thunderstorms

Thunderstorms sometimes occur, in particular over the northern half of the area, but they usually have a limited duration.

4. Coastal weather bulletins

VHF
Italian weather bulletin Ch 68
Continuous (in English and Italian)

Meteomar bulletins can also be received from following local emitters (their range varies, so it is advisable to try and listen to the various channels to detect which station provides local coverage):

SARDINIA

P. Campu Spina Ch 82 *0135, 0735, 1335, 1935 (Sardinian Sea, Sardinian channel, Central and Southern Tyrrhenian)*

Margine Rosso Ch 62 *0135, 0735, 1335, 1935 (Sardinian Sea, Sardinian channel, Central and Southern Tyrrhenian)*

Monte Serpeddi Ch 04 *0135, 0735, 1335, 1935 (Sardinian Sea, Sardinian channel, Central and Southern Tyrrhenian)*

Porto Cervo Ch 26 *0135, 0735, 1335, 1935 (Corsican sea, Sardinian Sea, Central Tyrrhenian)*

Monte Moro Ch 28 *0135, 0735, 1335, 1935 (Corsican Sea, Sardinian Sea, Central Tyrrhenian)*

Osilo Ch 26 *0135, 0735, 1335, 1935 (Corsican Sea, Sardinian Sea, Central Tyrrhenian)*

Cagliari Ch 25, 27 *0135, 0735, 1335, 1935 (Sardinian Sea, Sardinian channel, Central and Southern Tyrrhenian)*

Monte Limbara Ch 85 *0135, 0735, 1335, 1935 (Corsican Sea, Sardinian sea, Central Tyrrhenian)*

CONTINENTAL COAST AND ADJACENT ISLANDS

Zoagli Ch 27 *0135, 0735, 1335, 1935 (Corsican Sea, Ligurian Sea, Northern Tyrrhenian)*

Monte Bignone Ch 07 *0135, 0735, 1335, 1935 (Corsican Sea, Ligurian Sea, Northern Tyrrhenian)*

Castellaccio Ch 25 *0135, 0735, 1335, 1935 (Corsican Sea, Ligurian Sea, Northern Tyrrhenian)*

Gorgona Ch 26 0135, 0735, 1335, 1935 *(Ligurian Sea, Northern and Central Tyrrhenian)*

Monte Nero Ch 61 *0135, 0735, 1335, 1935 (Ligurian Sea, Northern and Central Tyrrhenian)*

Monte Argentario Ch 01 *0135, 0735, 1335, 1935 (Northern, Central and Southern Tyrrhenian)*

Torre Chiaruccia Ch 64 *0135, 0735, 1335, 1935 (Northern, Central and Southern Tyrrhenian)*

Monte Cavo Ch 25 0135, 0735, 1335, 1935 *(Northern, Central and Southern Tyrrhenian)*

Varco del Salice Ch 62 *0135, 0735, 1335, 1935 (Central and Southern Tyrrhenian)*

Posillipo Ch 01 *0135, 0735, 1335, 1935 (Central and Southern Tyrrhenian)*

Serra del Tuono Ch 25 *0135, 0735, 1335, 1935 (Central and Southern Tyrrhenian)*

Capri Ch 27 *0135, 0735, 1335, 1935 (Central and Southern Tyrrhenian)*

SICILY AND ADJACENT ISLANDS

Forte Spuria Ch 85 *(Southern Tyrrhenian, Northern and Southern Ionian)*

Sferracavallo Ch 27 *0135, 0735, 1335, 1935 (Southern Tyrrhenian, Sicily strait)*

...a Ch 84 *0135, 0735, 1335, 1935*
(Southern Tyrrhenian, Sicily strait)

Cefalu Ch 61 *0135, 0735, 1335, 1935*
(Southern Tyrrhenian, Sicily strait)

Pantelleria Ch 22 *0135, 0735, 1335, 1935*
(Southern Tyrrhenian, Sicily strait)

Erice Ch 81 *0135, 0735, 1335, 1935*
(Southern Tyrrhenian, Sicily strait)

Caltabellotta Ch 82 *0135, 0735, 1335, 1935*
(Sicily strait)

Gela Ch 26 *0135, 0735, 1335, 1935*
(Sicily strait)

Mazara del Vallo Ch 25 *0135, 0735, 1335, 1935*
(Sicily strait)

Campo Lato Alto Ch 86 *0135, 0735, 1335, 1935*
(Sicily strait and Southern Ionian)

Siracusa Ch 85 *0135, 0735, 1335, 1935*
(Sicily strait and Southern Ionian)

Lampedusa Ch 25 *0135, 0735, 1335, 1935*
(Sicily strait)

Grecale Ch 21 *0135, 0735, 1335, 1935*
(Sicily strait)

It should be noted that Meteomar is technically an offshore bulletin as it is related to wide sea areas, but the same text is also used for coastal forecasts. When sailing in areas where coastal features have a relevant impact on wind characteristics, it is advisable to keep in mind that the bulletin may not consider many of these local modifications, hence adjust accordingly the forecast contents.

Please note the area is also covered by several other services (Navtex, HF radio, Radiofax, etc): as most of them provide weather forecasts to several different areas, they have all been grouped at the end of the book.

See the Weather Forecast Appendix for more details.

Figure 4.E.1 Adriatic sea area

ADRIATIC SEA

1. Geographic features

This is the sea area to the east of Italy, usually divided into northern, central and southern Adriatic by weather forecast providers.

The southern boundary is represented by the strait of Otranto, separating the heel of the Italian boot from Albania and NW Greece. In the strait, winds from the NW or the SE are usually 40% higher than over the surrounding area.

The area is almost enclosed among mountain chains: the Alps to the N–NW, the Dinaric Alps to the East, and the Apennines to the West. Only a few major gaps exist: the Po valley and the Trieste gap being the two most important ones.

These characteristics have a deep influence over weather behaviour in the area.

2. Seasonal weather overview

Winter

Weather is often unsettled, the whole area being under the influence of repeated low pressure systems transiting over it, frequently inducing SE flows especially over the central and southern parts of the area.

Besides, an area of high pressure usually extends over the Balkans, creating frequent episodes of cold and violent northeasterly winds, especially over the northern part of the area.

Summer

The Açores high ridge extension towards the Italian peninsula, together with the weakening of the Balkans high usually bring fair, warm weather, with calms or light breezes.

Sea breezes along the western coast tend to veer from a NW/NE direction to SE at sunset; along the eastern shore they are usually more NW oriented (*see below, Maestrale*). Land breezes usually start after sunset, along the eastern shore of the Adriatic they tend to blow from the NE in the north and from the E in the south; along the western shore, they usually blow S to SW.

Gale force winds are possible but rare.

Spring and autumn

As in other Mediterranean areas, these seasons do not show a specific pattern, they are more transition periods between summer and winter-type weathers. During spring this transition usually takes two or three months, whereas during autumn it is generally more abrupt.

3. Weather features and winds

Gale force winds are relatively more frequent over the northern and southern thirds of the area, while in the central Adriatic they occur more rarely.

Low pressure systems

1. Genoa cyclones. *See the relevant section for characteristics and forecasting.*

    These depressions usually influence the area in two ways.

    If they form over the Po valley/Gulf of Venice and then drift NE through the Alps, sirocco conditions will be likely, especially if the low extends southward. *Figure 4.E.2.*

    Sometimes they may also drift SE through the Adriatic and deepen. This usually brings cyclonic circulation all over the area: Bora winds to the NE, NE to NW winds on the northwestern Adriatic, westerly winds along the southern coast of Italy, and sirocco winds along the SE Adriatic. *Figure 4.E.3.*

    If they form in the Genoa Gulf then move towards the Ionian/southern Adriatic, bora wind will be likely, *see Bora section below.*

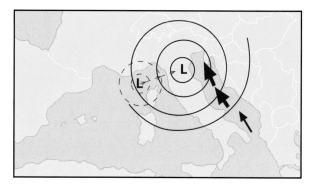

Figure 4.E.2 A Genoa low migrating towards the Alps with a trough extending to the south is likely to generate sirocco

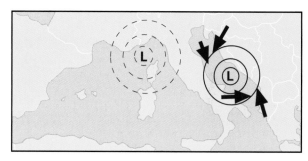

Figure 4.E.3 Genoa low drifting towards the Adriatic and associated wind distribution

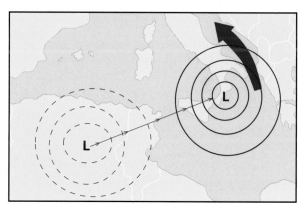

Figure 4.E.4 NWA depression causing sirocco in the Adriatic

2. NWA cyclones. *See the relevant section for characteristics and forecasting.*

    These depressions affect the area when they move northeastward from the Gulf of Gabes. They are rare during summer.

    When they arrive in a position west of the area, sirocco winds usually occur throughout the entire Adriatic, together with low level clouds, precipitations and often fog. *Figure 4.E.4.*

Bora

Bora is a north to northeasterly wind generated by a sudden pulse of cold Siberian air over the Dinaric Alps, which then spreads over the whole Adriatic Sea and sometimes beyond. Bora-like phenomena occur also in the Aegean Sea and eastern Mediterranean.

Its name may derive from the Greek Boreas, the north wind.

It is a cold, violent and gusty wind; speeds in excess of 100kn are not unheard of. It is a true katabatic wind, as it takes most of its strength from the fall of cold air accumulated over the Balkan mountains down from the eastern Adriatic mountain chains.

Formation and forecasting

Although ultimately the severity of bora episodes is usually determined by local, subsynoptic factors, some different large scale pressure features can be identified.

There are three main bora varieties associated with different pressure situations, although sometimes their features may be mixed.

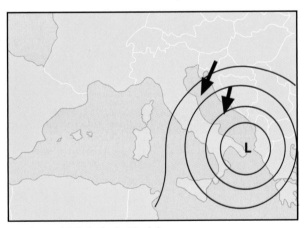

Figure 4.E.5 Cyclonic / Dark bora

Type A Cyclonic bora (also called Dark bora), Figure 4.E.5.: a depression located south of the Dinaric Alps (over the south Adriatic or Ionian Sea) creates a pressure gradient across the Adriatic eastern shore and air is drawn from the continent towards the sea.

Over the sea, pressure drops are often observed. The associated weather is usually cloudy and rainy, and the wind effects are usually felt over the whole Adriatic, although winds tend to be stronger over its southern half.

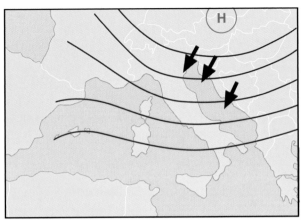

Figure 4.E.6 Anticyclonic / Clear bora

Type B Anticyclonic bora, Figure 4.E.6.: a strong high pressure area over central Europe extending towards the north or northeast of Italy generates a pressure gradient across the Dinaric Alps, often without any organized low pressure area to the south.

Air is somewhat 'pushed' from the continent towards the sea. Wind is most violent near the eastern Adriatic shore. Associated weather is mostly cloudless, hence its alternative name 'Clear bora'.

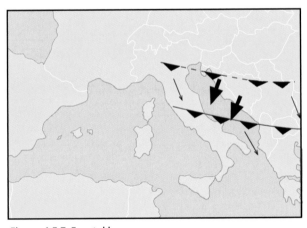

Figure 4.E.7 Frontal bora

Type C Frontal bora, Figure 4.E.7.: it is a violent squall created by the passage of a cold front across the area. If the temperature difference across the front is high, bora can be violent, but usually it will blow to gale to strong gale force, although its duration will usually be short.

A succession of cold fronts can cause repeated bora episodes, separated only by short periods of weaker winds. Frontal bora is usually strongest during winter.

Bora should be expected whenever a high pressure area is likely to build over the Balkans, and/or a depression is expected to move or develop) over the northern Ionian Sea (*see Ionian depressions section for more details*).

All three kinds of bora may last for several days.

Forecasting aids

Bora onset is near when white clouds become visible over the top of the coastal mountains of eastern Adriatic, and small cloudy fragments begin to descend from the mountains. If the clouds over the mountains thicken, bora is likely to grow in strength.

Direction and strength

Bora usually blows from the NE when it first enters the Adriatic, but with variations along the coast as valleys and mountain ranges are oriented in different directions.

On the eastern half of the Adriatic, the wind comes from the NE to the north, and tends to blow from an ENE–E direction further south.

In the middle of the sea, bora tends to blow from a N–NE direction.

On the western, Italian side of the Adriatic, it tends to back and come more from a N–NNW direction, particularly south of Ancona.

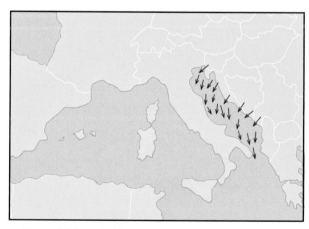

Figure 4.E.8 Typical bora orientation

Bora onset is sudden: the first gusts may quickly reach 25–35 knots in a matter of minutes, but the wind maximum speed is usually reached a few hours later.

Bora strength is at its maximum along the eastern coast of the Adriatic, more so to the north; it decreases towards the open sea and to the south.

Peak gust speeds are often at double the average wind speed.

Local features have a great influence on its speed. It tends to be stronger where mountain heights are above 500m and are directly over the sea, or where valleys and gaps open along the mountain range and channel the wind. It tends to be less strong where a plain lies between the base of the mountains and the sea shore. Ashore or over the islands, trees and vegetation leaning towards the S–SW usually indicate areas to be avoided.

Figure 4.E.9 shows the various areas where bora wind is locally stronger: A. Trieste Gulf, B. Kvarner Gulf, C. Velebit channel, D. Sibenik area, E. Split-Makarska, F. Peljesac-Korcula area, G. Dubrovnik.

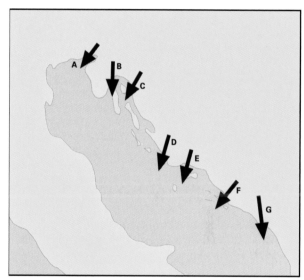

Figure 4.E.9 Areas of stronger bora

Locations where it blows with particular violence are Trieste, Karlobag, Rijeka, Senj, Kraljevica, Sibenik, Split, Makarska, Dubrovnik, Boka Kotorska and Ulcinj. It is slightly weaker downwind of Istria, Dugi otok, Kornati islands, Mljet island and Cavtat.

Bora is somewhat less intense (although gale or strong gale force winds are common) over the open Adriatic Sea.

Type A bora shows a greater frequency of gale force winds than Type B.

During the afternoons, especially in summer, thermal effects tend to reduce somewhat bora strength.

Forecasting aids

A 10hPa pressure difference between north and south Adriatic usually generates a gale force bora over the sea.

Wind speed reports at Italian coastal stations usually give a good approximation of wind speeds over the southwestern half of the Adriatic Sea.

Area of influence

Bora is most common over the Adriatic Sea, where it is originated.

Sometimes it remains localized to only a few miles distance along the eastern Adriatic coast (more frequently during summer), though most of the times it blows all over the Adriatic, commonly reaching as far as the northern Ionian Sea, especially if a strong depression is found over the Ionian Sea or southern Italy.

A particularly strong bora may cross the Apennine mountain chain and blow N to NE over the Tyrrhenian Sea as far as Corsica and Sardinia, where it is usually called Tramontana (*see relevant section*)

When a high pressure area extends over the Balkans, and a deep depression is located over the south central Mediterranean, bora can cross most of the Ionian and blow as far as Malta, although it will lose most of its violence and be much warmer and moist.

Seasonal and daily variation

Bora wind may occur at all seasons. It is most common during late autumn and winter (October–March), when it may last up to two weeks. On average, Trieste usually experiences a gale force bora six days or more per month; with an average duration of three days.

During summer, bora usually lasts two, three days at most, but there are also shorter episodes when it blows fiercely during just a few hours and then stops. On average, Trieste usually experiences a gale force bora one day or less per month, with an average duration of one day.

Although bora can start at any moment of the day, it is slightly more frequent in the afternoons than mornings; it blows with greater fury between 0800 and 1000 hours, and between 1800 and 2100; locally, thermal effects tend to reduce somewhat bora strength along the eastern coast of the Adriatic; the minimum speed along the coast usually occurs around midnight.

Cloudiness

When a depression is associated with a Type A bora, extensive low level cloudiness will develop over the Adriatic, together with light rain or drizzle. Snow may be an occurrence during the cold season.

With Type B bora, the cloud belt over the mountain tops of the eastern Adriatic will dissipate as wind blows downhill and skies will be clear, metallic, with impressive visibilities.

Cessation

The main synoptic factor suggesting an end to bora episodes is the weakening or displacement of the Balkan high pressure area.

Also, the increase of low level clouds is usually a sign of bora cessation.

With a Type A wind (dark bora) cessation is usually heralded by clearing skies to the NE.

Sirocco

See the relevant section for characteristics and forecasting.

Sirocco (sometimes called Jugo or Yugo along the eastern Adriatic) is usually associated with the warm sector of low pressure systems, either from the Gulf of Genoa or particularly from NWA (*see above*). It can often be forecast by pressure drops, especially over the northern part of the area, increasing cloudiness and humidity.

If in conjunction with a low pressure area located in the middle of the Adriatic (*see Genoa lows, above*), sirocco will be limited to the southern part of the area, and be associated with bora winds to the north, the boundary between the two areas often being around the island of Vis.

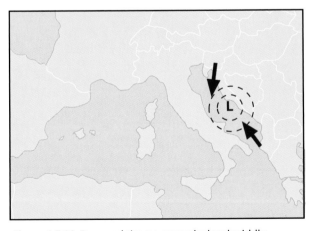

Figure 4.E.10 Bora and sirocco around a local middle Adriatic low

It is more frequent to the south, but sea conditions worsen with the longer fetch as it travels northward (especially north of the Palagruza island), where the low depth of the sea contributes to generate high waves. Over the north part of the area it is more frequent during spring and early summer, while to the south during autumn and winter.

Sirocco is usually announced during calm weather by developing haze to the SE; pressure begins to drop slowly, clouds thicken and begin drifting to the NW as the wind starts blowing.

The onset of the wind is gradual: its speed increases slowly, reaching a maximum between 36–48 hours after its beginning. It is usually weaker than bora, although gale or strong gale force siroccos are not uncommon, especially during winter and spring. Sea breeze effects tend to increase its speed during the afternoon, whereas it will be relatively weaker during the night. Sirocco duration is usually of two or three days, while the strongest winds usually last 12/24 hours.

Generally, a pressure difference of 10hPa from the north to the south of Italian eastern coast generates gale force sirocco. It is strongest when isobars on the eastern side of the area are packed.

It usually blows from the S–SE near the strait of Otranto (where it is accelerated by a channelling effect) and the southern half of the Adriatic, it spreads and reduces its speed as it travels north taking a more E–SE direction along the NW of the area, and SE along the NE part of the Adriatic.

Mlijet), and the coast around Dubrovnik. A 1·5–2kn NW surface current is often associated with sirocco.

Another type of sirocco, usually of more moderate speed, is called Anticyclonic sirocco, and may develop in association with a stable high pressure ridge to the east of the area, and depressions drifting NE over western Europe. In this case the weather is usually fine, with only high level clouds periodically covering the sky and with light rains which may develop after 36/48 hours. It is mainly a spring or autumn phenomenon.

Maestrale

It is the common name of the northwesterly summer breeze: it usually starts just before noon, then increases during the afternoon and dies at night. It usually blows at 4–5Bft, but channelling effects in the Otranto strait may increase its speed to gale force.

Apart from sea breeze effects, maestrale can be also be originated by a pressure configuration similar to the meltemi wind one (*see under Aegean Sea area*), of whom it may be considered a distant cousin: in this case it will usually blow all over the Adriatic as far as the Peloponnesus, and not be only confined to coastal areas.

Garbin

Garbin is the local name given to a SW wind often blowing to gale force usually over the central and southern portions of the area. It is mainly determined by the combined effect of a high

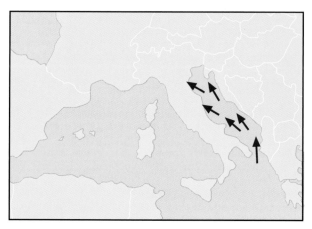

Figure 4.E.11 Typical sirocco orientation

Areas of particularly strong sirocco include the Gulf of Venice, the Kvarner Gulf, the channels between the outer Croatian islands (Vis, Lastovo,

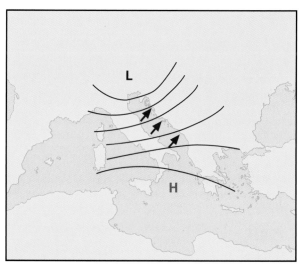

Figure 4.E.12 Typical surface pressure distribution leading to Garbin

pressure area to the S–SW of the area, and an eastward drifting low to the north.

It is usually announced by moderate southerly winds, a drop in pressure and the formation of a hazy area to the SW. The wind then veers SW and rapidly increases in strength. It generally subsides once pressure begins to rise and the low migrates farther to the east.

Depending on pressure distribution, garbin episodes may be followed by bora during the following 24–36 hours (*see above*).

Katabatic summer winds

During summer, the thermal contrast between the high mountains along the eastern Adriatic and the coast sometimes creates short episodes of katabatic wind comparable to bora in direction and strength. Although it can blow to gale or strong gale, it usually lasts no more than a few hours.

Thunderstorms and squalls

Thunderstorms are a common feature of the area and can often represent a danger to yachts.

They are frequent during the summer season (on average, 15 cases over the north Adriatic, 20 over the central eastern portion of the area, from 5 to 10 over the central western part and to the south), spring and autumn frequencies are roughly halved. They are rare during winter.

These groups of cells usually originate over NE Italy and then drift to the E or SE along the Adriatic and towards the Croatian coast (where they are often called Nevera) at a speed of 15–20kn. They bring strong to violent gusts, heavy rain, hail and intense lightning, but they usually last only a few hours.

Although difficult to forecast with much advance, the top of the cumulonimbus cloud is often visible from a certain distance by day, whereas at night the lightning can give and idea of their location and direction of movement. Pressure usually rapidly falls before its onset.

Once the thunderstorm has passed, if air temperature drops and wind tends to blow from the northerly quadrants, other episodes will be less likely; if on the other hand air temperature remains warm and light winds blow from E to SE, other cases may occur during the following hours or day.

Fog

The Adriatic being a rather shallow, relatively warm sea, fog is common during the cool season, especially when winds are light or calm.

4. Coastal weather bulletins

VHF

Italian weather bulletin Ch 68
Continuous - (All areas) - (in English and Italian)

Meteomar bulletins can also be received from the following local emitters (their range varies, so it is advisable to try and listen to the various channels to detect which station provides local coverage):

Abate Argento Ch 05 *0135, 0735, 1335, 1935*
(Northern Ionian and Southern Adriatic)

Bari Ch 27 0135, 0735, 1335, 1935
(Northern Ionian and Southern Adriatic)

Monte Calvario Ch 01 *0135, 0735, 1335, 1935*
(Southern and Central Adriatic)

Casa d'Orso Ch 81 *0135, 0735, 1335, 1935*
(Southern and Central Adriatic)

Silvi Ch 65 *0135, 0735, 1335, 1935*
(Southern and Central Adriatic)

Piancavallo Ch 01 *0135, 0735, 1335, 1935*
(Central and Northern Adriatic)

Monte Secco Ch 87 *0135, 0735, 1335, 1935*
(Central and Northern Adriatic)

Monte Conero Ch 02 *0135, 0735, 1335, 1935*
(Central and Northern Adriatic)

Porto Garibaldi Ch 25 *0135, 0735, 1335, 1935*
(Central and Northern Adriatic)

Monte Cero Ch 26 *0135, 0735, 1335, 1935*
(Central and Northern Adriatic)

Ravenna Ch 27 *0135, 0735, 1335, 1935*
(Central and Northern Adriatic)

Conconello Ch 83 *0135, 0735, 1335, 1935*
(Central and Northern Adriatic)

It should be noted that Meteomar is technically an offshore bulletin as it is related to wide sea areas, but the same text is also used for coastal forecasts. When sailing in areas where coastal features have a relevant impact on wind characteristics, it is advisable to keep in mind that the bulletin may not consider many of these local modifications, hence adjust accordingly the forecast contents.

STATIONS ALONG THE EASTERN COAST

Rijeka Ch 04 *(Kamenjak station, Rab island)*, 20 *(Susak station, Susak island)*, 24 *(Vrh Ucka station, Rijeka)*, 81 *(Savudrija station, NW Istria) 0535, 1435, 1935 Local Time*

Split Ch 07 *(Sv. Mihovil station, Ugljan island)*, 21 *(Labistica station, Split)*, 23 *(Vidova Gora station, Brac island)*, 28 *(Celavac station)*, 81 *(Hum station, Vis island) 0545, 1245, 1945 LT*

Dubrovnik Ch 04 *(Uljenje station, Peljesac)*, 07 *(Srdj station, Dubrovnik)*, 85 *(Hum station, Vis island 0625, 1320, 2120 LT*

Continuous weather forecasts are also locally available in Croatian, English, German and Italian, with three daily updates at 0700, 1300 and 1900 LT:

Pula Ch 73 *Northern Adriatic and west coast of Istria*

Rijeka Ch 69 *Croatian side of Northern Adriatic*

Split Ch 67 *Croatian side of Central Adriatic*

Dubrovnik Ch 73 *Croatian side of Southern Adriatic*

Bar Ch 20, 24 *0850, 1420, 2050*

Please note the area is also covered by several other services (Navtex, HF radio, Radiofax, etc): as most of them provide weather forecasts to several different areas, they have all been grouped at the end of the book..

See the Weather Forecast Appendix for more details.

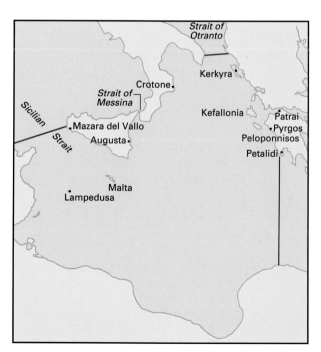

Figure 4.F.1 Ionian sea area

IONIAN SEA

1. Geographic features

This sea area covers the south central portion of the Mediterranean.

It is limited to the north by the three straits of Otranto, Messina and Sicily; to the east it is limited by meridian 022°E. Figure 4.F.1.

Corresponding GMDSS weather areas are Melita, Gabes, Boot, Sidra, North Ionio, South Ionio and the western half of Southwest Kritiko.

Mountain chains with an influence over the weather include the Atlas to the west (although out of the area, it is responsible for the generation of important low pressure systems), the Apennines and Sicily mountains to the north, mainland Greece and Peloponnesus mountains to the east.

As the fetch may be extended, high waves usually occur on the open sea during gale force situations.

Funnelling effects in the strait of Otranto usually increase wind speeds by 40% respect to coastal stations.

In the strait of Messina the channelling effect causes southerly or northerly winds to converge and then spread in a 'V' – 'inverted V' pattern, where their speed increases and usually causes high sea states.

2. Seasonal weather overview

The area is under the seasonal influence of the African desert and Eurasian air masses, with the added component of the pressure systems transiting over the sea.

Winter

The main determinants of bad weather are depressions, which may cause windy and sometimes stormy weather. Winds blowing around these systems are sirocco, mistral, gregale and bora.

Spring

Sahara desert heats up, NWA depressions develop and may cause extended episodes of gale force winds, mainly from the southern quadrants to the east, and NE to W to the west. Thunderstorms may sometimes occur.

Summer

Temperature gradients form between the sea and warm air over the northern land, and with the hotter Sahara to the south. Associated weather is usually warm; winds are generally light except for meltemi which may affect limited portions of the area.

Sea-land breezes are common along the shores. Around Sicily they tend to blow S to SW along its southern coast, and NE to SE along its eastern coast; along the Tunisian coast they are usually easterly, and can bring reduced visibilities; over the northern Ionian they tend to blow 2 to 5Bft from noon until sunset; around Malta they are usually light and variable.

Autumn

It is generally short lasting, with a swift passage from summer type weather to winter-like.

3. Weather features and winds

Low pressure systems

1. NWA depressions. *See the relevant section for characteristics and forecasting.*
   Depressions of this type affecting the area are mainly those which leave the Gulf of Gabes area and move northeast towards the Aegean Sea.
   Sirocco and gregale winds are the main associated winds.

2. Genoa depressions. *See the relevant section for characteristics and forecasting.*
   Genoa lows affecting the area are those moving SE, either parallel to the Italian west coast or across the Apennine towards the southern Adriatic. The low may become stationary or fill over the southern Tyrrhenian, in which case a secondary low usually develops over the northern Ionian.
   Associated winds are mainly sirocco and bora/gregale.
   If a strong bora episode is underway over the Adriatic, these lows may quickly deepen and cause stormy conditions along their path. *Figure 4.F.2*

3. Ionian Sea depression. *See the relevant section for characteristics and forecasting.*
   Mainly associated with bora outbreaks from the Adriatic, these depressions show similar characteristics to Genoa lows described above. They usually move S–SW and then curve to the east towards Crete.

Bora

See the relevant section for characteristics and forecasting.
   If it is limited to the Adriatic, the wind usually blows out of the strait of Otranto to the south for about 50/60M.

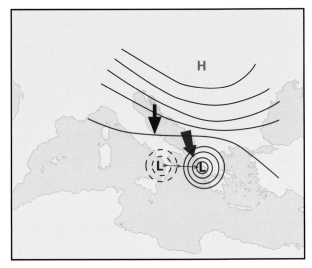

Figure 4.F.2 Deepening low associated with bora conditions

If it is associated with a depression transiting over the southern Ionian it usually blows from the northeast throughout most of the area, in which case it 'transforms' into gregale. *Figure 4.F.3.*

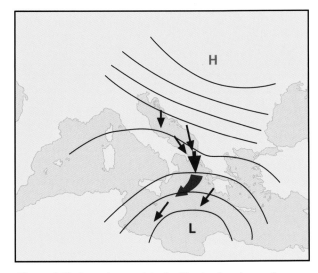

Figure 4.F.3 Gregale associated with a Ionian depression

Weather along the Greek coast is usually clear, with gusty winds; as the wind travels over the water it gathers moisture and gregale type weather develops, with clouds and precipitations.

Gregale

See the relevant section for characteristics and forecasting.

This strong NE wind usually occurs during winter, when on average 7–8 episodes usually occur.

It may blow at 6–7Bft for extended periods, and is usually associated with low level clouds and heavy precipitations. The long fetch causes high seas along the eastern coast of Sicily and the western Ionian islands (Malta, Lampedusa, etc).

Sirocco

See the relevant section for characteristics and forecasting.

Sirocco usually blows along with moving depressions, its direction is usually determined by isobars orientation, and may be from the SW to the SE. It is more likely during winter and spring.

It brings low level clouds, precipitations and sometimes fog, but its speed is usually lower than with other types of wind. During summer it is rare, but can reach the same strength as during the other seasons.

Mistral

See the relevant section for characteristics and forecasting.

This wind may occasionally blow as far as the central Ionian when an upper level trough over central Europe is associated to a ridge over the Atlantic ocean.

In this case, a strong southwestward flow may bring mistral through the strait of Sicily and to Malta: it is accelerated by the channelling effect and often blows to gale or strong gale force with gusts. Because of its long path over water, it is usually accompanied by precipitations. *See also Figure 4.D.2. under the Tyrrhenian area section.*

Maistro

See the Meltemi section under the Aegean Sea chapter for characteristics and forecasting.

Meltemi episodes over the Ionian are limited to the Ionian Greek coast, where the wind takes the name of Maistro. It usually blows from the NW and with less force than Aegean meltemi (4–5, occasionally 6Bft), although it is locally accelerated around and between the Greek Ionian islands.

It is a common occurrence during the summer months: any alterations of this regime should be considered with care as they may indicate worsening weather, especially when coupled with a drop in pressure.

Fog

Fog is usually limited to the early morning hours, especially during spring or early summer windless days. It usually disappears a few hours after sunrise.

4. Coastal weather bulletins

VHF

Italian weather bulletin *Ch 68 Continuous All areas (in English and Italian)*

Meteomar bulletins can also be received from the following local emitters (their range varies, so it is advisable to try and listen to the various channels to detect which station provides local coverage):

SICILY AND ADJACENT ISLANDS

Cefalu Ch 61 *0135, 0735, 1335, 1935 (Southern Tyrrhenian, Sicily strait)*

Pantelleria Ch 22 *0135, 0735, 1335, 1935 (Southern Tyrrhenian, Sicily strait)*

Erice Ch 81 *0135, 0735, 1335, 1935 (Southern Tyrrhenian, Sicily strait)*

Caltabellotta Ch 82 *0135, 0735, 1335, 1935 (Sicily strait)*

Gela Ch 26 *0135, 0735, 1335, 1935 (Sicily strait)*

Mazara del Vallo Ch 25 *0135, 0735, 1335, 1935 (Sicily strait)*

Campo Lato Alto Ch 86 *0135, 0735, 1335, 1935 (Sicily strait and Southern Ionian)*

Siracusa Ch 85 *0135, 0735, 1335, 1935 (Sicily strait and Southern Ionian)*

Lampedusa Ch 25 *0135, 0735, 1335, 1935 (Sicily strait)*

Grecale Ch 21 *0135, 0735, 1335, 1935 (Sicily strait)*

CONTINENTAL ITALIAN COAST

Ponta Stilo Ch 84 *0135, 0735, 1335, 1935 (Northern and Southern Ionian)*

Capo Colonna Ch 20 *0135, 0735, 1335, 1935 (Northern and Southern Ionian)*

Monte Parano Ch 26 *0135, 0735, 1335, 1935 (Northern and Southern Ionian)*

Capo Armi Ch 62 *0135, 0735, 1335, 1935 (Northern and Southern Ionian)*

Abate Argento Ch 05 *0135, 0735, 1335, 1935 (Northern Ionian and Southern Adriatic)*

It should be noted that Meteomar is technically an offshore bulletin as it is related to wide sea areas, but the same text is also used for coastal forecasts. When sailing in areas where coastal features have a relevant impact on wind characteristics, it is advisable to keep in mind that the bulletin may not consider many of these local modifications, hence adjust accordingly the forecast contents.

Malta Ch 04 *0603, 1003, 1603, 2103*

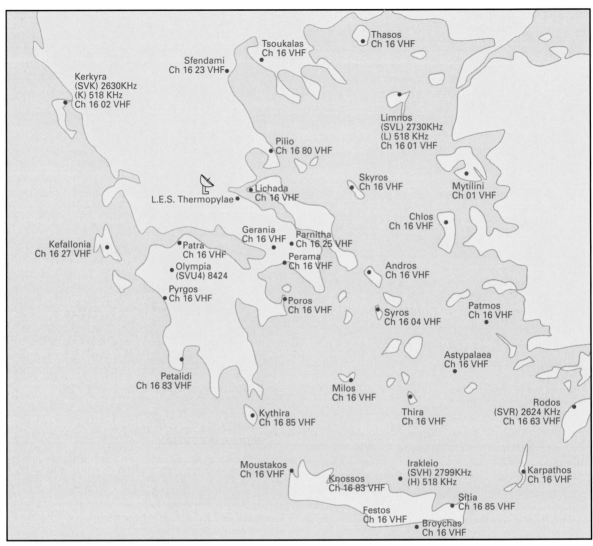

Location of Greek VHF stations

Source: Hellenic National Meteorological Service

Greek bulletin (Greek and English)

Local broadcast channel indicated after a general call on
Channel 16 *(See chart for local station locations)*

GREEK VHF STATIONS

Kefallonia Ch 27 *0600, 1000, 1600, 2000*

Kerkyra Ch 02 *0600, 1000, 1600, 2000*

Patra Ch 85 *0600, 1000, 1600, 2000*

Petalidi Ch 83 *0600, 1000, 1600, 2000*

Please note the area is also covered by several other
services (Navtex, HF radio, Radiofax, etc): as most of them
provide weather forecasts to several different areas, they
have all been grouped at the end of the book.

See the Weather Forecast Appendix for more details.

AEGEAN SEA

1. Geographic features

The area is limited to the south by meridian 022°E, parallel 35°N, and meridian 030°E, and to the north by the Marmara Sea.

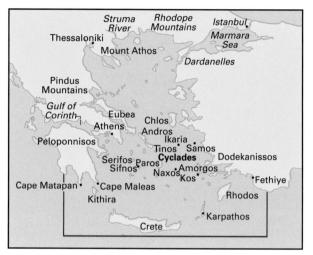

Figure 4.G.1 Aegean sea area

It is usually sub-divided into sixteen smaller areas by the weather forecast providers.

Orographic features abound, clockwise from Peloponnesus mountains we find the Gulf of Corinth, then the Pindus mountains which end at the Vardar gap, this valley and the adjacent Struma River are separated from the Marmara Sea by the Rhodope mountains. To the east are the mountains of the Turkish peninsula, to the south the Cretan island relief.

Several dozen islands are scattered in the middle of the area, and cause the typical funnelling, relief and corner effects over the winds.

2. Seasonal weather overview

Winter

A strong thermal contrast exists between cold air over the Balkans area and the relatively warmer sea surface.

This may help the development or re-fuelling of frontal and low pressure systems, causing bad weather with precipitations all over the area, or else the cold air may invade the Aegean with gale force winds from the N to NE.

The frequency of gale force winds is among the highest of the Mediterranean, with no statistically prevalent direction.

Spring

During April and May, the weather usually alternates between a winter-type one, and a dryer, finer weather typical of summers. Meltemi wind isn't usually experienced until the month of June.

Summer

A trough of the monsoonal low pressure area over southwest Asia extends over Turkey, interacting with a higher pressure area to the west: strong north to northwest winds are the typical feature of Aegean summers. Whenever meltemi does not blow, weather is usually dry and settled.

Autumn

Summer-type weather usually lasts well into the month of September, whereas during October the transition to winter characteristics usually takes place. Meltemi has stopped blowing, but episodes of cold, strong N–NE winds are possible, together with periods of unsettled weather caused by low pressure systems over the area.

3. Weather features and winds

Low pressure systems

Depressions have a strong influence over the weather especially during the period from October to April/May, while they are less likely in the remaining part of the year.

The strong thermal gradient between land and sea increases the likelihood of gale to strong gale winds around the lows.

1. NWA Cyclones. *See the relevant section for characteristics and forecasting.*

These lows are likely to cross over the Aegean from the southern Mediterranean if pressure over Turkey is less than 1000hPa.

If not, most of them stop once they arrive over the northern Ionian, generally causing the development of an Aegean low.

When they transit over the area, these depressions usually bring gale to strong gale winds. Sirocco is a common occurrence before the passage of the low centre, and increasing S to SE winds over the southern Aegean give a good indication of the likely passage of a depression. Cold winds from the northern sectors usually follow, often with increased strength.

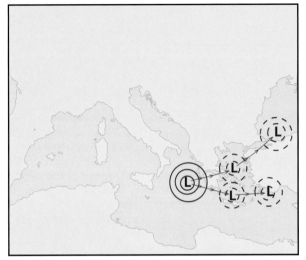

Figure 4.G.2 Ionian sea depressions over the Aegean area

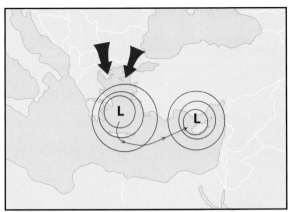

Figure 4.G.3 Southern Aegean – Cretan sea depressions

2. Ionian Sea Cyclones. *See the relevant section for characteristics and forecasting. Figure 4.G.2*

These lows sometimes appear to fill when they arrive west of Greece: particular care should be taken as a secondary low usually develops over the Aegean. Its usual trajectory is NE, towards the Black Sea.

Whenever the area is under a cold air influx from the north, depressions from the Ionian usually follow a more southerly path, transiting over Peloponnesus, Crete and southern Turkey.

3. Southern Aegean Sea - Cretan Sea Cyclones

These depressions are often related to Genoa/Ionian lows that have either migrated into the area, or have remained stationary along the west coast of Greece, inducing secondary low development over the Aegean Sea.

Their formation is more likely during autumn and winter.

They often develop when the Aegean Sea is subject to an intense northerly cold air flow (*see below*). In this case, the low may drift south or southwest for a short period of time and then curve towards the northeastern Mediterranean. The strongest winds are usually found on the northern side of these systems, which also bring heavy precipitations. *Figure 4.G.3*

On upper level charts, a 500hPa trough with its axis orientated NE–SW over the Balkans is a feature often related to the development of an Aegean depression. *Figure 4.G.4*

Sirocco wind is the typical feature announcing Aegean cyclones (especially if the low

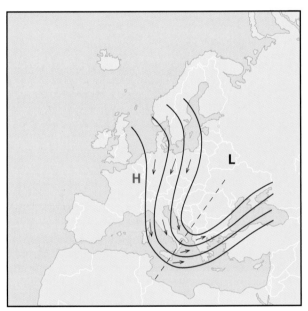

Figure 4.G.4 Upper level contours likely to lead to Aegean low development

pressure area reaches into North Africa), but gale and strong gale force winds are more likely to the West and to the Northern quadrants of the cyclone.

Precipitation can be intense during the passage of the fronts associated with the low.

Meltemi

The meltemi is a seasonal, monsoonal NE to NW wind blowing over the Aegean Sea and sometimes eastern Mediterranean. Also called Etesian (a word of Greek origin), it is a typical summer to early autumn wind.

Meltemi can be a good ally for navigation: it is seasonal, its direction is well predictable, it is associated with good weather and it cools down the very hot Greek summers, nonetheless if it usually blows 5 to 7Bft, it can easily reach 7–8 or 9Bft, so especially with smaller size boats care must be taken, not only while sailing but also at anchor, where terrain features can increase its strength.

Formation and forecasting

Basically, meltemi is originated by the combination of two semi-stable pressure features drawing continental air from northeastern Europe into the Mediterranean: to the west the Açores high ridge often extending over the Mediterranean, to the east the low pressure area located over the Persian Gulf and Middle East (the same low pressure area creating the Asian monsoon). To a smaller scale, two low pressure areas (one over the Turkish peninsula/Middle east, and/or a Cyprus depression) interact with a higher pressure area over the Balkans.

1. Meltemi is likely when the Balkan high pressure centre is situated over the indicated area, and its associated ridge extends southward through the Aegean.

Figure 4.G.5 A high pressure centred inside the boxed area with a ridge extending to the south are likely to generate meltemi

2. Meltemi is likely if a trough from the Middle East/Cyprus lows extends into the southern Aegean area indicated in the figure.

Figure 4.G.6 A surface trough extending from the E into the boxed area will probably generate meltemi

3. Meltemi is likely if 500hPa charts show a strong ridge located over western Europe, and a strong trough affects the Aegean region indicated on the figure, possibly with upper air winds speed of 30 knots or more.

Figure 4.G.7 500hPa contours usually leading to meltemi

If the trough is stable and does not move much, meltemi is likely to last several days. If on the other hand 500hPa flow shows a succession of troughs and ridges over the area, meltemi is more likely to blow in shorter spells of a couple of days.

4. In general, meltemi is likely whenever forecast surface charts indicate building high pressure over the Balkans and cyclogenesis over the Turkish peninsula.

5. Meltemi is also likely after the south or southeastward passage of a cold front over the Aegean.

6. Meltemi onset is sometimes announced 12/36 hours in advance by a slow pressure rise (4hPa in 12 hours is sometimes reported), a humidity drop and the development of fragmented mid to high level clouds. This is especially true during the months of July and August.

7. It is reported that meltemi development is not likely if pressure at Cyprus is above 1009hPa.

8. During May–June and September–October, especially along the coastal areas, meltemi is often preceded by one day of thunderstorms, which may last a few more hours until the wind is well established.

Area, direction and strength

Meltemi extends from Dardanelles and the northern Aegean Sea southeastward into the eastern Mediterranean, and to a limited area to the southwest of Peloponnesus. Strong meltemi episodes may be felt as far as the Egyptian coast to the south, and Israel and Lebanon to the east.

Average monthly wind speed and directions are shown in Figure 4.G.8.

Dashed lines represent wind directions, solid lines represent percentages of average winds 6Bft or higher. These are average speeds: gusts and local effects are likely to generate stronger winds (*see below*).

From a northerly direction over the northern and central Aegean (meltemi blows out of Dardanelles more from the NE), wind usually backs to a more NW to W direction over the Dodecanese islands, around the Turkish peninsula and the eastern Mediterranean.

Gale or strong gale force meltemi is more likely to be found along a line running from the northeastern Aegean to slightly east of Limnos and Skiros islands, through the Cyclades, then towards the area

between Rhodes and Karpathos, and eventually in the northern East Mediterranean (where wind speeds are likely to be lower).

Another area of relatively stronger meltemi is the southwest coast of Peloponnesus, where it usually blows more from a northwesterly direction.

If coastal station reports are available, pressure differences of 7–8hPa between Rhodes and Istanbul, or of 6hPa between Rhodes and Athens are both likely to indicate gale force meltemi over the Aegean Sea.

Local features are also likely to increase its speed and gustiness:

1. Channelling effects produced by the various geographic Aegean features:

a. in the Doro channel, between Andros and Eubea, meltemi will likely increase by 1–2 Beaufort notches (and create a strong southerly sea current which makes the strait almost impassable northward for sailing boats);

b. between the Dodecanese islands and the Turkish peninsula (where an opposed current creates steeper and sometimes breaking seas),

c. among the Cycladic islands (especially Paros, Naxos and Mykonos);

d. between Ikaria and Samos;

e. between Karpathos and Crete.

2. Fall wind effects: meltemi speed increases downwind of the islands of Euboea, Tinos, Andros, Pholegandros, Amorgos, Serifos, Sifnos, Kea and Kos.

In the lee of Crete island, meltemi may create gusty, foehn-type winds of gale force; altocumulus lenticularis over Cretan mountains are usually a good indication of winds along the south coast of more than 6Bft, especially in front of valleys. Over the sea area between the eastern limit of Crete and Rhodes, wind force is usually 1Bft notch higher than along the northern Cretan coast, with stronger gusts.

A strong meltemi can sometimes create a local closed area of low pressure over Rhodes island, where the wind can be greatly reduced.

Figure 4.G.8 (opposite) Meltemi monthly average speed and direction. Solid lines indicate percentages of winds of 6Bft or higher. Dashed lines represent directions

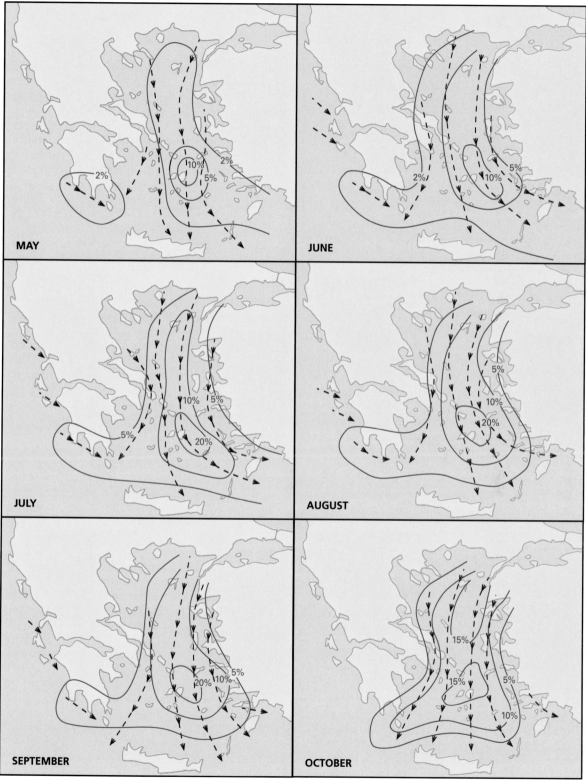

MAY

JUNE

JULY

AUGUST

SEPTEMBER

OCTOBER

- - ► Wind direction ——— Percentage of winds

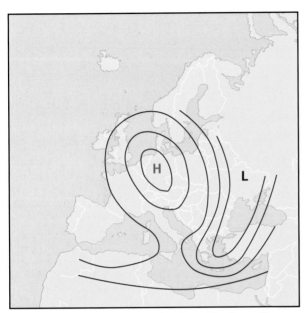

Figure 4.G.9 An upper level blocking ridge is usually associated with long lasting meltemi

Duration

Meltemi will likely last for several days when 500hPa winds are of northerly direction, and in particular if a deep, stable low is over the Black Sea (indicated by both surface and upper level charts).

Likewise, an extended period of meltemi is likely when upper air charts show a blocking ridge over central Europe. *Figure 4.G.9.*

Conversely, meltemi will blow in a series of short spells of a few days duration when 500hPa charts indicate a shallow, limited amplitude trough/ridge situation, with upper level wind flow mainly of westerly direction.

Monthly and daily variations

Meltemi is essentially a summer wind. It only blows from May to October, but the highest number of occurrences with a peak in frequency and strength is during the months of July and August.

On average, gale force winds occur only between 3–7 days during the month of May or June, between 10 and 14 days during July and August, and 5–7 days during October.

The average duration of meltemi gale force episodes is roughly a couple of days during May, June or October: during these months, it usually starts at 4–5Bft, slowly reaches 6–7 or more, then decreases. Gale force duration is longer during July and August, where it usually lasts four or five days

but can continue up to ten days, with calm periods in between lasting a couple of days. September is more a transition month.

A weak meltemi usually starts around noon, builds to 4–5Bft and then subsides at night.

A strong meltemi on the other hand can reach 6–7Bft (more under local features effects) and keep on blowing for a few days.

Sea breeze effects have a marked influence over meltemi when it blows at a maximum 5 or 6Bft. Along the west coast of Greece, from the Ionian islands southward to Peloponnesus, meltemi is absent or relatively weaker: sea breezes blow W to NW 4–5Bft by noon, and increase up to 5–6Bft in the late afternoon. Wind usually disappears at night.

At Athens, meltemi strength is lowest around midday, when local sea breeze effect is from the opposite direction.

Over the northern Aegean, maximum wind speeds tend to occur in the early afternoon, whereas over the southern half they tend to happen a few hours later, around 1500–1600. In this area, meltemi sometimes disappears at night (but not as a rule), although sailing may still be uncomfortable because of the swell.

Over the eastern Aegean, near Turkey, the sea breeze effect tends to increase meltemi strength, whose maximum speed is usually reached around 1700–1800.

Sea waves

Meltemi is associated with steep seas, which can be high in the central Aegean.

On the lee of the smaller islands, the shelter is somewhat reduced by the swell circling around the land.

Cloudiness

Meltemi is usually associated with clear skies and good visibilities.

Fragmented altocumulus may forewarn of a meltemi outbreak in an otherwise cloudless sky, and convective clouds may develop later over the top of mountain features, especially over the southern Aegean islands where the wind arrives with higher humidity content.

If a meltemi is associated with the passage of a cold front, thunderstorms may develop both before and after the frontal transit. They are more likely during spring and autumn, and usually limited to the northern half of the Aegean; they are rare south of Athens.

Figure 4.G.10 A ridge drifting over the Aegean will usually stop meltemi

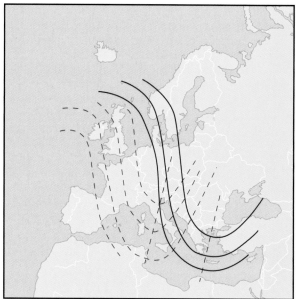

Figure 4.G.11 Upper level features likely to generate northerlies over the Aegean

During late spring and early autumn, thunderstorms may occur also without any atmospheric disturbance, and meltemi usually develops the following day.

Cessation

Meltemi will likely end when an upper level ridge is forecast to move over the southern Aegean, thus replacing the existing trough which will drift eastward or weaken. *Figure 4.G.10*

Meltemi will likely end if mistral conditions begin to appear.

Northerly winds – Vardar winds or Vardarac

See also the Bora section under Adriatic Sea area for related information.

These Bora-type winds are a common occurrence over the Aegean Sea, especially during winter. (Northerly meltemi winds are a typical summer phenomenon and are a different type of wind, *see above*.)

These winds may be associated with two different pressure distributions.

Type A occurs when the N to NE flow is shallow, meaning it can only be detected on pressure surface charts but not on upper level charts.

Type B occurs when the flow is deep, and can be seen on both surface and upper level charts.

Formation and forecasting

Strong, cold northerly winds are likely when these conditions prevail:

a. An area of high pressure is located over the Balkans and NW Greece, with a strong ridge extending southward over the Aegean. This is usually more likely during autumn and winter, less during spring when the high is usually rather weak.

b. A low pressure area is centred over the southern half of the Aegean Sea. This is an almost certain sign of northerly onset during winter and spring, less during autumn.

c. From upper level charts, the eastward movement of a ridge over the eastern Atlantic and a trough over central Europe are useful indications of the likelihood of strong northerlies. *Figure 4.G.11*

Isolated cold fronts are often associated with northerly wind streaks. They may bring periods of several days of bad weather all over the Aegean, as they often become stationary over the southern Aegean, around the island of Crete.

Direction and strength

When isobars orientation favours a northeasterly wind, it will usually enter the Aegean from the Dardanelles/Bosphorus straits, where it will be stronger.

When isobars orientation favours a northerly flow, the wind will mainly blow from the Vardar valley, to the north of Thessaloniki Gulf, where it is usually called Vardarac.

Going southward, the wind will usually back to a more northwesterly direction by the time it reaches the Dodecanese islands and the southwestern coast of Turkey.

It will be usually northerly over Crete island, and its speed usually strongly accelerated (1·5 to 2·5 times) along the southern coast of the island. Increased speeds are also common in the area between western Crete and the Peloponnesus.

Locally, wind direction is modified by features like islands, channels, although the general pattern is similar to that of meltemi winds.

Area of influence

The extension of northerly winds depends upon the cold air flow characteristics.

With a Type A flow, or if a depression is transiting over the south Aegean, the southward limit of these winds will likely be the island of Crete. While strong northwesterly winds will blow over the open sea, relatively sheltered areas will be found in the Gulf of Patras, Gulf of Corynth and in the lee of Euboea.

With a Type B flow, northerlies will likely spread as far as the eastern Mediterranean, where they usually back to a WNW direction.

Wind will be particularly strong and gusty in the lee of mountainous regions: cape Matapan (southern Peloponnesus), mount Athos, the island of Crete, Pelion peninsula, the Gulfs of Patras, Corynth and Thermaikos. In the Cyclads area, the stronger winds will be found in the channels between them and in the lee of mountainous islands.

Sea waves

These winds usually cause high, steep waves even over the northern part of the area.

Cloudiness

With a Type A flow, increased cloudiness, precipitations and low visibilities are to be expected.

With a Type B flow, the weather is usually fine, with clear skies over the Aegean, but as air travels over warmer water it will load with moisture and possibly generate convective clouds and sparse precipitations over the eastern Mediterranean.

Cessation

These winds usually end when the synoptic patterns which generated them weaken or disappear (*see above*). In particular, northerly are likely to stop blowing when the high pressure over the Balkans weakens or moves eastward, when the low pressure over the southern Aegean fills or moves away from the area, or if the 500hPa ridge axis transits over the Aegean.

Sirocco

See the relevant section for characteristics and forecasting.

As usual, this wind is associated with migrating depressions in eastward transit over the Aegean, and mainly affects the southern and western Aegean. Its frequency is highest from late autumn until spring.

It usually reaches no more than gale force, but wind speed may be greatly accelerated by channelling effect, especially between the Cycladic islands, or between the Dodecanese archipelago and Turkey.

Precipitations can be heavy, visibilities are usually reduced.

Fog

Over the northern Aegean, persistent fog (lasting a couple of days) may occur from late autumn to early spring when calm winds accompany a high pressure ridge from the Balkans.

Elsewhere, fog is usually limited to the early morning hours, especially during spring or early summer windless days. It usually disappears a few hours after sunrise.

4. Coastal weather bulletins

VHF
General call on Ch 16, followed by indication of local channel for weather broadcast (Greek and English). See chart for local station positions.

GREEK VHF STATIONS
Chios Ch 85 *0600, 1000, 1600, 2000*
Knossos Ch 83 *0600, 1000, 1600, 2000*
Kythira Ch 85 *0600, 1000, 1600, 2000*
Limnos Ch 82 *0600, 1000, 1600, 2000*
Moustakos Ch 04 *0600, 1000, 1600, 2000*
Mytilini Ch 01 *0600, 1000, 1600, 2000*
Parnis Ch 25 *0600, 1000, 1600, 2000*
Patra Ch 85 *0600, 1000, 1600, 2000*

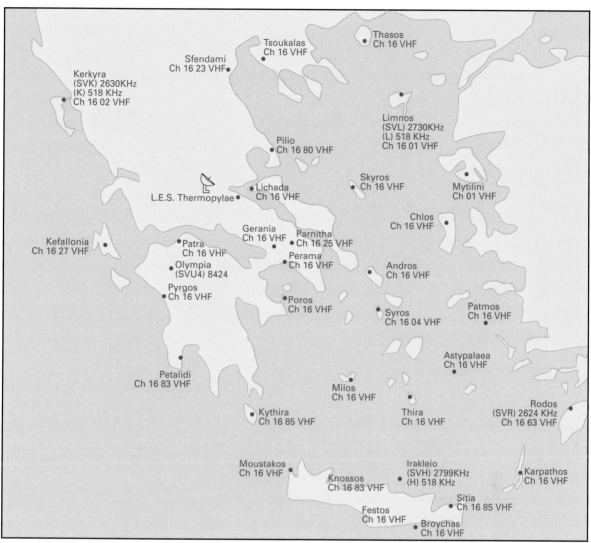

Location of Greek VHF stations

Source: Hellenic National Meteorological Service

Petalidi Ch 83 *0600, 1000, 1600, 2000*
Pilio Ch 60 *0600, 1000, 1600, 2000*
Rhodos Ch 63 *0600, 1000, 1600, 2000*
Sitia Ch 85 *0600, 1000, 1600, 2000*
Syros Ch 04 *0600, 1000, 1600, 2000*
Sfendami Ch 23 *0600, 1000, 1600, 2000*

Istanbul Ch 67 *0700, 1900 Several repeater stations (Turkish and English) (Marmara and Aegean Sea)*

Istanbul Ch 67 *0900, 1200, 1500, 1800, 2100 (Local time, advanced one hour during daylight saving time periods) (Coastal bulletins for Northern Aegean and Marmara).*

Please note the area is also covered by several other services (Navtex, HF radio, Radiofax, etc): as most of them provide weather forecasts to several different areas, they have all been grouped at the end of the book.

See the Weather Forecast Appendix for more details.

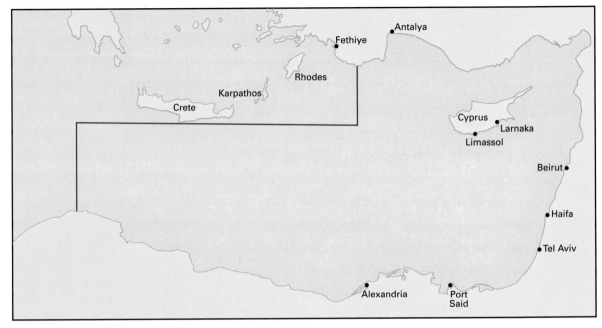

Figure 4.H.1 Eastern Mediterranean sea area

EASTERN MEDITERRANEAN

1. Geographic features

This area is limited by the NE Africa and Middle east coasts to the south, east and northeast, and to the NW by meridian 030°E, parallel 35°N and meridian 022°E. Figure 4.H.1.

It includes GMDSS weather areas Kastellorizo, Taurus, Crusade, Delta, Southeast Kritiko Ierapetra and the eastern portion of Southwest Kritiko.

The main geographic features from a meteorological point of view are the mountains of the Turkish peninsula, along the northern edge of the area, with only a couple of valleys opening to the sea, and the desert areas to the southern and southeastern boundaries. Along the eastern coast (Syria, Lebanon, Israel, etc.) there are only hills which do not constitute a particular barrier to wind flow.

Corner, funnelling and obstacle effects are common over Crete, around capes of the southern coast of Turkey, and around Cyprus island.

2. Seasonal weather overview

The region is under the influence of the monsoonal behaviour of the air over southwestern Asia and southeastern Europe.

Winter

Depressions from the west usually move inside a corridor established by the Eurasian high pressure area to the north, and the Sahara high to the south. They usually affect the northern half of the area, and as thermal differences between sea and land are big, strong winds, bad weather and heavy precipitations are frequent.

Spring

Spring weather is similar to summer, with the exception of incursions from NWA depressions transiting over the area.

Summer

The SW Asia low pressure system extends over Turkey, westerly winds develop all over the area, with a tendency to blow form the NW in the western half of the area; the weather is usually fine, with few precipitations. Winds are usually light to moderate, with the occasional outburst of meltemi. Along Israel and Lebanon coasts, sea breezes are usually light, and come from the westerly sectors; along the Egyptian shore they usually blow from the northerly sectors, at 3–4Bft. Around Cyprus, thermal low development may reinforce local breezes up to 5, occasionally 6Bft in the afternoon, although wind quickly abates at sunset.

Occasionally, a strong N–S pressure gradient over Asia minor may cause short episodes of northeasterly dry, hot winds from the mountains: these usually do not last long.

Autumn

It is a short season, usually characterized by the rapid change from summer-like weather to winter-type.

3. Weather features and winds

Low pressure systems

1. Cyprus Depressions
These lows usually form in the region south of the Turkish peninsula, roughly to the west of the island of Cyprus.

Figure 4.H.2 Cyprus depression at surface level

They are more likely from late autumn to early spring (with a peak during December, January and February), although not unknown during the remaining part of the year.
The underlying factors of cyclogenesis in the Cyprus area are similar to those of the Genoa lows.

a. An intense flow of cold air approaches the area from the northern sectors. When invested by such a northerly flow, the mountain chain of Asia Minor usually induces lee cyclogenesis to the south, over the sea.

b. Likewise, the same process happens with the southward movement of a cold front over Asia Minor.

c. Land and sea have different thermal characteristics, and often show marked contrasts, which contributes to cyclogenesis.

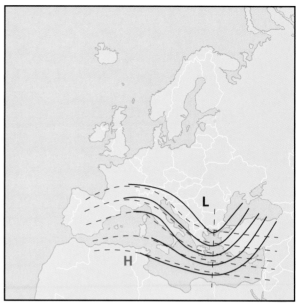

Figure 4.H.3 At upper level, a ridge over Western Europe (dashed lines) may subsequently lead to trough formation over the Aegean (solid lines) which will support Cyprus depression development

Upper level charts (Figure 4.H.3) initially show just a ridge over western Europe, while over the area a zonal flow prevails (dashed lines); in the following day, a trough develops over the Aegean and a Cyprus low rapidly deepens. The low usually fills when the trough axis drifts eastward.
An approaching Cyprus lows may bring warm and rainy sirocco winds on its eastern side, whereas to the west, after the passage of the low centre gale to strong gale force gusty winds develop, with thunderstorms and very intense precipitations.
The low may remain stationary along the southern coast of Turkey for as long as a week, in which case the repeated formations of small troughs around the low cause stronger northeasterly winds to alternate with weaker northwesterlies.

2. Southern Aegean and Ionian Sea depressions. *See the relevant sections for characteristics and forecasting.*
Although sometimes of different origin, once these lows arrive over the area they show a very similar behaviour.
Whenever these systems drift southward or generate in the region around the island of Crete, they tend to proceed eastward towards Cyprus, affecting the whole northern half of the area. *Figure 4.H.4 overleaf*

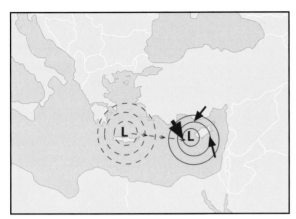

Figure 4.H.4 Southern Aegean and Ionian sea depressions typical path

Under these depressions, the strongest winds are usually found to the north and to the west, especially after the passage of an associated cold front.

3. NWA lows. *See the relevant section for characteristics and forecasting.*

Particular care should be taken with systems migrating eastward on land, along the northern coast of Africa, especially during spring (sometimes called Sharav depressions), which may curve to the northeast and cause strong winds over the whole eastern Mediterranean.

Meltemi – Northerly winds

See the relevant sections of the Aegean Sea chapter for characteristics and forecasting.

A particularly strong meltemi in the Aegean may extend southeast towards the eastern Mediterranean, where its speed will be reduced the farther it travels from the Aegean. Its direction tends to be W–WNW along the south coast of Turkey and around Cyprus island. Associated weather is usually fair, with only limited development of convective clouds.

Similarly, outside of the summer season, northerly winds associated with a deep cold air flow may affect the area. They tend to blow from the WNW, and cause increasing cloudiness and showers towards the eastern edge of the area. Gale force winds are rare.

Katabatic summer winds.

During summer, the thermal contrast between the high mountains of the Turkish peninsula and its southern coast sometimes creates short episodes of strong NE to NW katabatic wind. Although it can blow to gale or strong gale, it usually lasts no more than a few hours.

Sirocco

See the relevant section for characteristics and forecasting.

Over the northern portion of the eastern Mediterranean, it is usually associated with the eastern sector of all the low pressure systems travelling over the area, and occurs more frequently from late autumn to spring.

Over the southern part of the area, it is more frequent during spring, in association with eastward migrating NWA lows. It may blow from SE to SW, and while temperatures may be very high, gale force winds are occasional, and often confined to the first 40–50 miles from the African or Middle eastern coasts.

Over the southeastern parts of the area, when associated with Sharav depressions it tends to blow from the E to SE, drawing hot air from the Arabian desert.

Fog

Fog may occur during the early morning hours, especially during spring or early summer windless days. It usually disappears a few hours after sunrise.

4. Coastal Weather bulletins

VHF

Antalya Ch 67 *0700, 1900 From several repeater stations (Turkish and English) (Marmara, Aegean and Mediterranean Sea)*

Cyprus Larnaca and Limassol radio stations may give weather forecasts after a call on Ch 16 (usual working channels are 24, 25, 26 and 27)

Inshore forecasts for the day are also issued by FM Radio 1 Cyprus on 89.7MHz, 92.1MHz and 99.6MHz; approximate Local Times are 0640, 1015, 1310.

Haifa Ch 24, 25, 26 *Weather forecast on demand after a call on Ch 16 for areas Delta, Crusade, Taurus.*

Syria Two stations are reported
Latakia Ch 13 *0400, 0800, 1200, 1600, 2000, 2400*
Tartous Ch 20 *0400, 0800, 1200, 1600*

Please note the area is also covered by several other services (Navtex, HF radio, Radiofax, etc): as most of them provide weather forecasts to several different areas, they have all been grouped at the end of the book.

See the Weather Forecast Appendix for more details.

APPENDIX I

How to get weather information

There are many services providing weather forecasts, either for the whole Mediterranean or significant portions of it.

The more local providers (mainly coastal VHF stations) have been indicated under each Sea Area chapter; below is a list of several other services offering varying geographic coverage, spanning from just a couple of Mediterranean areas to the whole of the sea.

The technical means used are very diverse, and new ways of disseminating weather information are introduced on a regular basis.

Voice Radio - Radiotelephony weather bulletins are available practically everywhere, often in English. They can be received with a marine VHF radio, a shortwave (H.F.) receiver, or a home radio for local FM and AM stations.

Navtex broadcasters abound in the Mediterranean, and generally offshore forecasts for each sea area can be obtained by different stations. Reception depends on propagation and physical location (it can be more difficult when sheltered by high mountains, or when near big cities or ports with a lot of electromagnetic noise), but it is usually good over the whole sea.

HF Marine and Amateur nets are not so developed as in other areas of the world, still a few of them show a varying degree of activity in the Mediterranean too.

Radio Fax broadcasters offer a practical way of getting weather charts when on the open sea, either by a dedicated receiver or by means of an SSB radio, a computer and decoding software. The listed stations and schedules provide different kind of charts for Europe and the Mediterranean in particular.

RTTY Radio Teletype transmissions are made by the German Hamburg Pinneberg station. They issue 5-day text weather forecasts both in German and English, and user reports are generally good.

Internet is the quickest developing weather information channel: on a daily basis new sites are added, existing ones increase or modify their content, etc.; sometimes their relative value is similar and the preference for one of them rather than another becomes a question of personal taste as to the way information is displayed or made available. The list below indicates National Met Office internet sites (generally the main generators of primary meteorological information), other general providers of primary or derived information, and finally the main sites where high resolution charts can be found.

Many of these sites also describe varying offers of weather services not strictly related with web browsing, to mention just a few among a growing offer: WAP access to forecasts, fax services, email services, forecasts by SMS, phone services, etc.

GRIB files are an efficient way of transferring weather information (like actual or forecast wind speed, pressure, sea state, etc.), in particular through very compact email messages. Although some caution is necessary with their interpretation, they are more and more widespread, especially among cruisers using electronic charting/routing systems.

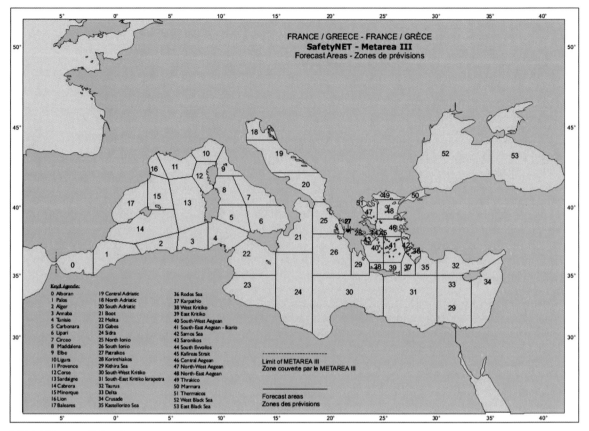

Official Metarea III Sea Areas

Inmarsat terminals or satellite phones are other important sources of weather information, but as they are used by a very limited amount of cruisers, they have not been considered.

Finally, a few examples of different national coastal bulletins are reported, together with a description of their usual structure.

As a reference, official Metarea III forecast areas are indicated in the above chart. However, as a few National Met Offices use their own sea areas, other relevant maps can be found below.

An important reminder

Whenever weather information is accessed, it is of the foremost importance to:

1. Always check the time and date of every product. For forecasts, consider also how many hours are left between the present time and the forecasting horizon shown on the chart. A 24 hour forecast based on a 0000 chart is of limited value if only available in the afternoon.

2. Always check what the primary source is: which Organisation original data comes from, which model is used (global or meso-scale), what kind of data treatment has been done by the provider (interpolations etc.) etc.

In the following schedules, time is UTC except where indicated.

RADIOTELEPHONY - VOICE RADIO

SPAIN STATIONS

Chipiona 1656kHz *0733, 1233, 1933 (in Spanish)*
Tarifa 1704kHz *0733, 1233, 1933 (in Spanish)*
Cabo de Gata 1767kHz *0750, 1303, 1950 (in Spanish)*
Palma de Mallorca 1755kHz *0750, 1303, 1950 (in Spanish)*

Spanish Offshore sea areas are the same as shown in the Figure above, though some names are spelt a bit differently (notably Cerdeña for Sardaigne/Sardinia, Córcega for Corse/Corsica, or Argelia for Alger).

Spanish Offshore bulletins usually contain a 'Clave MAFOR', a 5-digit number summing up all the forecast for a given area, which can be useful in cases of bad reception.

MAFOR code takes the form '1GDFmWm' ; where the first '1' digit is fixed. If G=5 forecasts are valid over 18 hours, if G=6 forecasts are valid for 24 hour. The meaning of the other digits is explained in the table below.

MAFOR Number	D Wind direction	Fm Wind strength (Bft)	Wm Other weather elements
0	Calm	0–3	Visibility >3M
1	NE	4	Risk of ice on superstructures (Air T between 0°C and -5°C)
2	E	5	Strong risk of ice on superstructures (Air T < -5°C)
3	SE	6	Mist (visibility 0·5M to M)
4	S	7	Fog (visibility <0·5M)
5	SW	8	Drizzle
6	W	9	Rain
7	NW	10	Snow, or rain and snow
8	N	11	Squally weather, with or without showers
9	Variable	12	Thunderstorms

For example, a MAFOR code 15749 means:

1   a fixed digit, can be disregarded as it does not say anything about the forecast
5   Forecast valid 18 hours (see above)
7   Northwesterly wind (to be read under the second column, marked D)
4   Wind strength 7Bft (to be read under the third column, marked Fm)
9   Thunderstorms (to be read under the fourth column, marked Wm)

MOROCCO STATION
Tanger 2635kHz *h+03mins (in French)*

FRANCE AND MONACO STATIONS

CROSS La Garde 1696kHz and 2677kHz *0650, 1433, 1850 Local time.*
Gale warnings in English and French are repeated every four hours, at 0103, 0503, 0903, 1303, 1703, 2103 local time. (Bulletins cover Est Cabrera, Minorque, Provence, Corse, Maddalena, Baleares, Lion, Ligure, Sardaigne and Elba sea areas)

France Inter 162kHz *around 2003 Local time (in French)*
(Same sea areas as CROSS Station)

France Info 1557kHz or 1242kHz *0645 Local time (in French)*
(Same sea areas as CROSS Station)

France Bleue Marseille 1242kHz *around 0640 Local Time (in French)*
(Same sea areas as CROSS Station)

France Bleue Nice 1557 kHz *around 0640 Local Time (in French)*
(Same sea areas as CROSS Station)

Monaco Radio Ch 403 and 804 (On-board receive frequencies 4363kHz and 8728kHz)
*(in English and French) 0930, 1403, 1930 Local time. Forecasts for western
Mediterranean*

Monaco Radio Ch 403, 804 and 1224 (On-board receive frequencies 4363kHz,
8728kHz and 13146kHz) *(in English and French) 1030 UTC. Forecasts for the eastern
Mediterranean*

ITALY STATIONS
All stations broadcast in Italian and English

Cagliari 2680kHz *0135, 0735, 1335, 1935*
(Sardinian channel, Sardinian Sea, Corsican Sea)

Augusta 2628kHz *0135, 0735, 1335, 1935*
(Sicily strait, Ionian Sea, Southern Adriatic)

Porto Torres 2719kHz *0135, 0735, 1335, 1935*
(Corsican Sea, Sardinian Sea, Central Tyrrhenian Sea)

Ancona 2656kHz *0135, 0735, 1335, 1935*
(Northern and Central Adriatic)

Genova 2722kHz *0135, 0735, 1335, 1935*
(Ligurian Sea, Northern Tyrrhenian, Corsican Sea)

Livorno 2591kHz *0135, 0735, 1335, 1935*
(Ligurian Sea, Northern and Central Tyrrhenian Sea)

Civitavecchia 1888kHz *0135, 0735, 1335, 1935*
(Northern and Central Tyrrhenian Sea)

Napoli 2632kHz *0135, 0735, 1335, 1935*
(Central and Southern Tyrrhenian Sea)

Messina 2789kHz *0135, 0735, 1335, 1935*
(Southern Tyrrhenian, Northern and Southern Ionian)

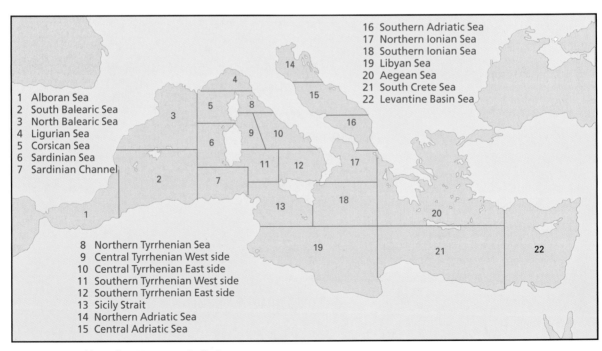

16 Southern Adriatic Sea
17 Northern Ionian Sea
18 Southern Ionian Sea
19 Libyan Sea
20 Aegean Sea
21 South Crete Sea
22 Levantine Basin Sea

1 Alboran Sea
2 South Balearic Sea
3 North Balearic Sea
4 Ligurian Sea
5 Corsican Sea
6 Sardinian Sea
7 Sardinian Channel

8 Northern Tyrrhenian Sea
9 Central Tyrrhenian West side
10 Central Tyrrhenian East side
11 Southern Tyrrhenian West side
12 Southern Tyrrhenian East side
13 Sicily Strait
14 Northern Adriatic Sea
15 Central Adriatic Sea

Sea Areas used by Italian Meteomar Bulletins

Palermo 1852kHz *0135, 0735, 1335, 1935*
(Southern Tyrrhenian Sea, Sicily channel)

Mazara del Vallo 2600kHz *0135, 0735, 1335, 1935*
(Sicily channel)

Lampedusa 1876kHz *0135, 0735, 1335, 1935*
(Sicily channel)

Crotone 2663kHz *0135, 0735, 1335, 1935*
(Northern and Southern Ionian)

Bari 2579kHz 0135, 0735, 1335, 1935
(Southern Adriatic, Northern and Southern Ionian, Sicily channel)

San Benedetto del Tronto 1855kHz *0135, 0735, 1335, 1935 (Central Adriatic)*

Trieste 2624kHz *0135, 0735, 1335, 1935 (Northern and Central Adriatic)*

Times may sometimes be shifted to 0150, 0750, 1350, 1950 UTC

Italian RAI I and RAI II broadcast weather forecast on several AM and FM frequencies a couple of times a day, their timetables differ depending on location and day of the week.

Among the possible frequencies on AM: 568, 675, 846, 936, 1035, 1062, 1116, 1431, 1449kHz. Likely timetables 0640, 1540, 1900, 2240 all LT.

The latest frequencies and times can usually be found on local newspapers.

Italian Meteomar bulletin sea areas are different from the GMDSS grid, their names are indicated opposite.

MALTA

Malta 2625kHz *0603, 1003, 1603, 2103*
(Waters inside a 50nm radius around Malta)

ALGERIA

Alger 1792kHz *0903, 1703 (French and English)*

Alger 2691kHz *0918, 2118*

Annaba *1911kHz 0850, 1850 (French and English)*

Oran 1735kHz *0835, 1835 (French and English)*

Radio TV Algerie 890kHz, 1304kHz, 11715kHz *1300, 2000 (in French)*

TUNISIA

Tunis 1820kHz and 2670kHz *0805, 1705 (in French)*

La Goulette 1743kHz *0405, 1905 (in French)*

Radio TV Tunis 629kHz, 962kHz, 7225kHz, 11970kHz and 15225kHz *0500 or 0600 (in French)*

CROATIA

Dubrovnik 2615kHz *0625, 1320, 2120*
(Croatian and English)

Rijeka 2771kHz *0535, 1435, 1935*
(Croatian and English)

Radio Zagreb 790kHz, 840kHz, 96.1MHz, 98.5Mhz *0900, 1230, 1900 (in English)*

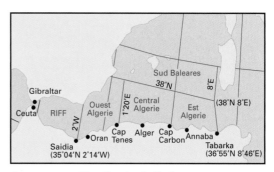

Sea areas used by Algerian bulletins

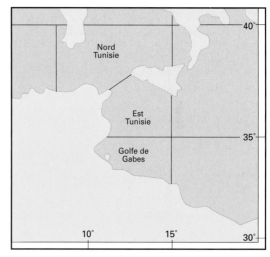

Sea areas used by Tunisian bulletins

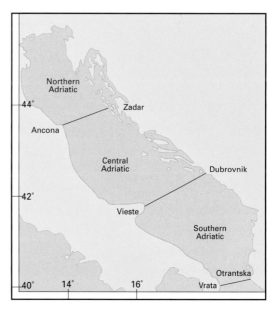

Sea areas used by Croatian bulletins

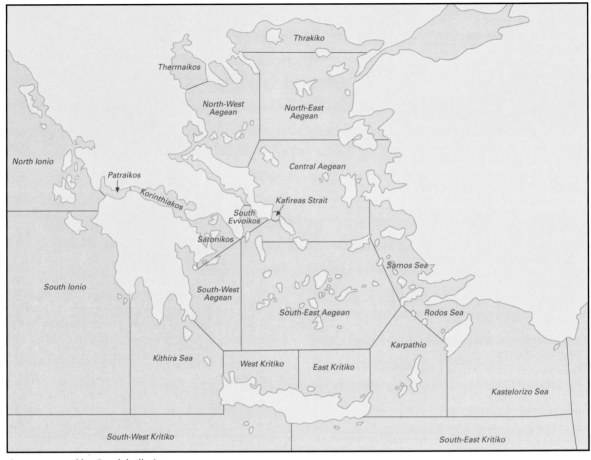

Sea areas used by Greek bulletins

MONTENEGRO

Bar 1720kHz *0850, 1420, 2050*
(Serb and English) (Adriatic Sea)

GREECE STATIONS

Kerkyra 2830kHz *0703, 0903, 1533, 2133*
(Ionian Sea)

Iraklion 2799kHz *0703, 0903, 1533, 2133*

Rhodos 2624kHz *0703, 0903, 1533, 2133*
(Eastern Greek waters and Eastern Mediterranean)

Khios 1820kHz *0703, 0903, 1533, 2133*

Limnos 2730kHz *0703, 0903, 1533, 2133*

Athina 2590kHz *0703, 0903, 1533, 2133*

Athina 4342kHz and 8681kHz *0348, 0618, 0948, 1518, 2118*

Athina 8735kHz *1215, 2015*

Athina/Voice of America 1590kHz *every full hour*

Greek bulletins use GMDSS Metarea III Forecast Areas, on page 84. The above chart details the Aegean Sea areas.

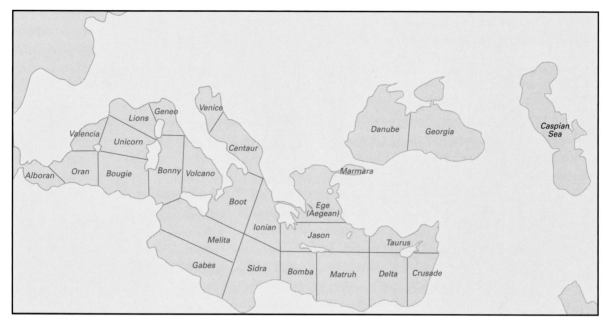

Sea areas used by Turkish bulletins

TURKEY STATIONS
Istanbul 4405kHz (Ch 417), 8812kHz (Ch 832), 13128kHz (Ch 1218) *1000, 1800*
Turkey Radio 6900kHz *0500, 0950, 1200, 1650 (altern. 0840, 1430, 1850 Local Time)*
Turkish National Radio FM 96.00MHz *0900 Local Time*

CYPRUS
Cyprus 2700kHz *0733, 1533 (Eastern Mediterranean)*

LIBYA
Tripoli 2197kHz *0833, 1733 (Area between 10°E and 25°E and Libyan coast to 34°N)*

ISRAEL
Haifa 2649kHz *on request, for areas Delta, Taurus, Crusade*

SYRIA
Latakia 3624kHz *0400, 0800, 1200, 1600, 2000, 2400*
Tartous 2662kHz *0400, 0800, 1200, 1600*

RADIO NETS

Although not so common as in other parts of the world, there are some radio nets serving the Mediterranean too, usually relaying weather information from official sources to cruisers equipped with SSB radios.

On amateur frequencies, the most reliable ones are:

UK Maritime Mobile net 14303kHz
0800 and 1800 UTC

Italian Amateur Radio Maritime Service 14297kHz *1900 UTC (English spoken)*

Sometimes other more or less regular contacts between 'ham' cruisers are made on the 7MHz band too.

Nets on the marine bands are somewhat less organized: they often have a higher regularity during summer while they sometimes disappear during winter. Frequencies vary too, but are usually centred on the 8MHz marine band: 8104kHz, 8122kHz and 8131kHz being among the ones used. They are usually held in the morning, around 0530–0600 UTC.

NAVTEX

Navtex stations broadcasting Offshore bulletins for Metarea III have the following Identification Letters; they operate in English on 518kHz. Their coverage usually spans over several Sea Areas and is sometimes modified, so rather than choosing the stations beforehand, it is advisable to avoid filtering the transmitters during one or two days: the receiver will list all the received messages, and then the most useful stations can be selected.

Croatia Split – Q – (Adriatic Sea and Strait of Otranto).

Cyprus Cyprus – M – (Eastern Mediterranean)

Egypt Alexandria – N – (Areas A, B, C and D, boundaries are shown in the chart below)

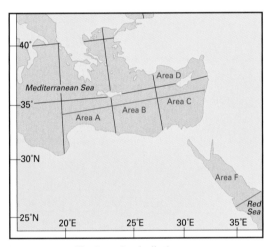

Sea areas used by Egyptian bulletins

France CROSS La Garde – W
(Est Cabrera, Minorque, Provence, Corse, Maddalena, Baleares, Lion, Ligure, Sardaigne and Elbe areas) (CROSS La Garde also issues bulletins in French on 490kHz, Identification Letter S)

Greece Heraklion – H
(Aegean Sea, Eastern Mediterranean)

Greece Kerkyra – K
(South Adriatic, North Ionian, South Ionian, Patraikos, Korinthiakos, Kithira Sea)

Greece Lemnos – L
(Aegean Sea, Marmara, Black Sea)

Israel Haifa – P
(SE Kritiko Ierapetra/Matruh, Delta, Taurus, Crusade)

Italy Rome – R
(Europe, North Africa, Near East)

These are the standard abbreviations used in Navtex messages

Abbreviation	Description
BACK	Backing
BECMG	Becoming
BLDN	Building
C-FRONT or CFNT	Cold Front
DECR	Decreasing
DPN	Deepening
E	East
EXP	Expected
FCST	Forecast
FLN	Filling
FLW	Following
FM	From
FRQ	Frequent
HPA	HectoPascal
HVY	Heavy
IMPR	Improve(ing)
INCR	Increasing
INTSF	Intensify(ing)
ISOL	Isolated
KMH	Km/h
KN	Knots
LAT/LONG	Latitude/Longitude
LOC	Locally
m	Metres
M	Nautical miles
MET	Meteo ...
MOD	Moderate
MOV or MVG	Moving/Move
N	North
NC	No change
NE	Northeast
NOSIG	No significant change
NW	Northwest
NXT	Next
OCNL	Occasionally
O-FRONT or OFNT	Occluded Front
POSS	Possible
PROB	Probable
QCKY	Quickly
QSTNR	Quasi-Stationary
QUAD	Quadrant
RPDY	Rapidly
S	South
SCT	Scattered
SE	Southeast
SEV or SVR	Severe
SHWRS or SH	Showers
SIG	Significant
SLGT or SLT	Slight
SLWY	Slowly
STNR	Stationary
STRG	Strong
SW	Southwest
TEMPO	Temporarily
TEND	Further outlooks
VEER	Veering
VIS	Visibility
VRB	Variable
W	West
W-FRONT or WFNT	Warm Front
WKN	Weakening

Italy Augusta – V
(Sicily strait, Ionian Sea, Southern Adriatic)

Italy Cagliari – T
(Sardinian channel, Sardinian Sea, Corsican Sea)

Italy Trieste – U
(Northern and Central Adriatic Sea)

Malta Malta – O
(Waters in a 50nm radius around Malta)

Spain Cabo de la Nao – X
(Western Mediterranean Sea)

Spain Tarifa – G
(Alboran, Palos and Algeria areas)

Turkey Istanbul – D
(Marmara and Danube areas)

Turkey Antalya – F
(Taurus area)

Turkey Izmir – I
(Aegean and Jason areas)

RADIOFAX

Actual and forecast graphic weather charts for Europe and the whole Mediterranean can be obtained aboard by means of a dedicated receiver, or by a HF radio connected to a simple PC with audio card and decoding software.

Hamburg / Pinneberg, Germany

Frequencies 3855kHz, 7880kHz, 13882.5kHz -- +/- 425Hz

The updated timetable for the emissions can be found at this internet address
www.dwd.de/de/wir/Geschaeftsfelder/Seeschifffahrt/ Sendeplaene/Sendeplaene.htm

Current schedule is as follows:

H are Heights
T is temperature
P is pressure
U is Humidity

0430 – Surface weather chart
0512 – h+30, Surface P
0525 – Surface pressure analysis, arrows showing the movement of pressure systems, significant weather.
0559 – h+12, h+24, 500hPa H+T, Surface P
0612 – h+12, h+24, 850hPa T, 700hPa U
0625 – h+36, h+48, 500hPa H+T, surface P
0638 – h+36, h+48, 850hPa T, 700hPa U
0651 – h+60, h+72, 500hPa H+T, surface P
0704 – h+60, h+72, 850hPa T, 700hPa U
0717 – Repetition chart 0512 UTC
0730 – h+48, surface P
0743 – Repetition chart 0525
0804 – h+84, surface P
0817 – h+108 surface P
0830 – h+24, Sea, swell and wind characteristics
0842 – h+48, Sea, swell and wind characteristics
0854 – h+72, Sea, swell and wind characteristics
0906 – h+96, Sea, swell and wind characteristics
1029 – h+48 wave predictions
1050 – Surface weather chart
1111 – Transmission schedule
1145 – Repetition chart 1050 UTC
1600 – Surface weather chart
1800 – Surface pressure analysis, arrows showing the movement of pressure systems, significant weather
1834 – h+24, Surface P
1837 – h+48, Surface P
1900 – h+84, Surface P
1913 – h+24, Sea, swell and wind characteristics
1926 – h+48, Sea, swell and wind characteristics
1939 – h+72, Sea, swell and wind characteristics
2137 – h+48, Wave predictions
2200 – Surface weather chart

Northwood, UK

Frequencies 2618.5kHz, 4610kHz, 8040kHz, 11086.5kHz

0000/1200	SFC ANALYSIS
0012/1212	SFC PRONOSIS T+24
0024/1224	850MB WEBT/PPTN T+24
0036/1236	OAT AND TD CONTOUR T+24
0048/1248	SHIP ICE ACCRETION
0100/1300	MAIN SCHEDULE
0124/1324	QSL REPORT
0136/1336	OCEAN FRONTS
0148/1348	300MB GPH
0212/——	SYMBOLOGY
——/1400	SEA SURFACE TEMP T+12
0236/1436	SFC ANALYSIS
0300/1500	SFC ANALYSIS
0348/1548	GALE WARNING SUMMARY
0400/1600	SFC ANALYSIS
0412/1612	OAT AND TC CONTOUR T+24
0424/1624	850MB WEBT/PPTN T+24
0436/1636	SURFACE PROGNOSIS T+24
0448/1648	SCEXA TAFS
0500/1700	SFC ANALYSIS
0512/1712	SURFACE PROGNOSIS T+24
0524/1724	SURFACE PROGNOSIS T+48
0536/1736	SCEXA TAFS
0548/1748	GALE WARNING SUMMARY
0600/1800	SFC ANALYSIS
0612/1812	SURFACE PROGNOSIS T+24
0624/1824	JMC T+12
0636/1836	JMC T+24
0648/1848	SCEXA TAFS
0700/1900	SPARE SCEXA TAFS
0712/1912	SIG WINDS T+24
0724/1924	SFC PROGNOSIS T+48
0736/1936	SFC PROGNOSIS T+72
0748/1948	SFC PROGNOSIS T+96
0800/2000	SFC PROGNOSIS T+120
0812/2012	THICKNESS/GPH ANALYSIS
0824/2024	SIG WINDS T+48
0836/2036	SIG WINDS T+72
0848/2048	SIG WINDS T+96
0900/2100	SFC ANALYSIS
0912/2112	TICKNESS/GPH ANALYSIS
0924/2124	THICKNESS/GPH ANALYSIS
0936/2136	850MB SPOT WINDS T+24
0948/2148	700MB SPOT WINDS T+24
1000/2200	SFC ANALYSIS
1012/2212	SURFACE PROGNOSIS T+24
1024/2224	REDUCED VIS T+24
1036/2236	850MB WEBT/PPTN T+24
1048/2248	OAT AND TD CONTOUR T+24
1100/ 2300	SFC ANALYSIS
1112/2312	SURFACE PROGNOSIS T+24
1124/2324	SEA AND SWELL T+24
1136/2336	THICKNESS/GPH T+24
1148/2348	GALE WARNING SUMMARY

Athens, Greece

Frequencies 4481kHz, 8105kHz

0845 –	Surface analysis for Southern Europe and the Mediterranean
0857 –	Surface analysis h+24 for Southern Europe and the Mediterranean
0909 –	Surface analysis h+48 for Southern Europe and the Mediterranean
0921 –	Wave height h+30 for the Mediterranean
0933 –	Wave height h+36 for the Mediterranean
0945 –	Wave height h+42 for the Mediterranean
0957 –	Wave height h+48 for the Mediterranean
1009 –	Wave height h+30 for the Aegean
1021 –	Wave height h+36 for the Aegean
1033 –	Wave height h+42 for the Aegean
1044 –	Wave height h+48 for the Aegean

Rome, Italy

Frequencies 4777.5kHz, 8146.6kHz, 13597.4kHz

0400 –	500hPa analysis
0415 or 0457 –	Surface analysis 0000 UTC (hour depends on daylight saving period)
0859 –	500hPa h+36
0906 –	500hPa h+48
0913 –	500hPa h+72
0920 –	500hPa h+96
0927 –	500hPa h+120
1030 –	Surface forecast h+24
1045 –	Surface analysis 0600 UTC
1153 –	Mediterranean Sea conditions
1645 –	Surface analysis 1200 UTC
1700 –	500hPa analysis
2230 –	Mediterranean Sea conditions
2312 –	Surface analysis 1800 UTC
2322 –	Surface forecast h+24

Reception of Athens and Rome stations is often patchy.

These schedules are sometimes modified and/or updated: a full, usually updated list can be found at the internet address:

www.nws.noaa.gov/om/marine/rfax.pdf

Otherwise, as many services usually transmit their full schedule of products at least once a day, in case of need it is barely sufficient to try and receive all radiofaxes during one full day to retrieve the one indicating available products and related timetables.

RADIO TELETYPE - RTTY

Hamburg Pinneberg daily issues 5-day text forecasts for the whole Mediterranean through radio teletype; user reports are usually very positive.

Again, these can easily be obtained aboard either by a dedicated receiver, or by means of a HF radio connected to a PC with audio card and decoding software.

The transmission schedule can change from time to time, the updated timetable can be found at www.dwd.de/de/wir/Geschaeftsfelder/Seeschifffa hrt/Sendeplaene/Sendeplaene.htm

Current schedule for the Mediterranean is as follows:

1. On frequencies 147.3kHz – 11039kHz – 14467.3kHz; emission at 50 Baud, +/-225Hz (except +/-42.5Hz for 147.3kHz)
German language service

0130 – Station reports
0135 – Medium range weather report. Weather situation and time series forecast for 5 days
0430 – Station reports
0535 – Medium range weather report
0730 – Station reports
0840 – Weather report Western Mediterranean Sea. Route Alboran–Tunis. Weather situation and time series forecast for 2 days
0930 – Weather report Eastern Mediterranean Sea. Route Eastern Tunis-Rhodes/Cyprus. Weather situation and time series forecast for 2 days.
1030 – Station reports
1120 – Medium range weather report
1330 – Station reports
1440 – Repetition weather report Western Mediterranean
1530 – Repetition weather report Eastern Mediterranean
1610 – Weather report. Weather situation and forecast valid for 24 hours
1630 – Station reports
1735 – Repetition medium range weather report
1930 – Station reports
2040 – Weather report Western Mediterranean
2130 – Weather report Eastern Mediterranean
2230 – Station reports

2. On frequencies 4583kHz, 7646kHz, 10100.8kHz; emission at 50 Baud, +/-225Hz.
English language service

0415 – Medium range weather report. Weather situation and time series forecast for 5 days.
1015 – Weather report Western Mediterranean
1115 – Weather report Eastern Mediterranean
1550 – Weather report. Weather situation and forecast valid for 24 hours
1610 – Medium range weather report
2215 – Weather report Western Mediterranean
2315 – Weather report Eastern Mediterranean

Sea areas differ somewhat from GMDSS ones, they are shown in the figure below.

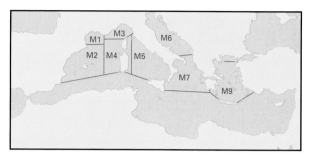

M1   Golfe du Lion
M2   Balearen
M3   Ligurisches Meer
M4   Westlich Korsika-Sardinien
M5   Tyrrhenisches Meer
M6   Adria
M7   Ionisches Meer
M9   Ägäis

Sea areas used by German bulletins

INTERNET

There is an ever increasing number of sites devoted to meteorology and it would be impossible to consider them all.

Weather sites usually offer different types of information: some of them are run by original data producers (like most National Met Office sites), while others compile and rearrange information to suit their various readerships.

Access is completely free for some of them, while others allow free-access to limited parts of their sites and offer a (more or less) wide range of subscription services (SMS forecasts, email services, WAP access, etc).

Here is a list of several of the most interesting sites for the Mediterranean.

As new content keeps on being added, and the structure and offer of every site is modified every now and then, if the reported link does not work, try and access the root directory and browse from there.

National Met Office sites

www.metoffice.gov.uk/weather/europe/surface_pressure.html
Surface pressure charts from the UK Met Office

www.meteo.fr
Meteo France official site. Text bulletins, pressure, wind, sea state charts, etc. Also, details about subscription service Navimail (*see below*)

www.dwd.de
German Met office site

www.dwd.de/de/WundK/W_aktuell/Seewetter/seewett_mm.html
Text forecasts for the whole Mediterranean, divided by area
www.dwd.de/de/WundK/W_aktuell/Seewetter/
Weather charts

www.hnms.gr/hnms/english/navigation/navigation_html
The Greek Met office site. Forecasts for Central and Eastern Mediterranean

www.inm.es
www.inm.es/web/infmet/predi/metmar/indpuer1.html
The Spanish Met office site. Text bulletins and Hi-Res charts for the Western Mediterranean

www.gencat.net/servmet/marcs/marc_mar.html
Cataluny a Met office site. Forecasts for Costa Brava, Costa Central and Costa Dorada of Catalunya

www.meteoam.it
Italian Met office site. Pressure charts with 2hPa spacing for the Central/Western Mediterranean (look for 'Situazione barica al suolo') and text bulletins for the whole Mediterranean (look for 'Meteomar')
www.meteoam.it/modules.php?name=Meteomar&scelta=Meteomar&lang=eng
www.meteoam.it/modules.php?name=viewImagesMeteoSat&fileName=satelliti/nefo/sfuk.gif&frame=75
Lightning activity

http://meteo.hr/index–en.php
Croatian Met Office site: text forecasts and Hi-Res charts for the Adriatic from Aladin high resolution model

www.maltairport.com/weather/page.asp?p=5472&l=1&lng=e&t=5
Malta Airport weather site. Charts and three day marine text forecasts

www.meteor.gov.tr/2006/english/eng-seamarine.aspx
The Turkish Met office site. Text bulletins and charts for the whole Mediterranean

www.ims.gov.il/imseng/all–tahazit
Israel Met office site

www.moa.gov.cy/moa/ms/ms.nsf
Cyprus Met office site. Also indicates eastern Mediterranean NAVTEX Forecast

www.jometeo.gov.jo
Jordan Met office site

www.meteo.cg.yu
Montenegro Met office site

www.arso.gov.si
Slovenian Met office site

www.meteo.dz
Algerian Met office site

www.meteo.tn
Tunisian Met office site

General Sites

www.ecmwf.int
Medium term forecasts from the European Centre for Medium Range Weather Forecasts

http://wxmaps.org/pix/euro.fcst.html
Short to Medium term charts from the US National Center for Environmental Prediction (NCEP)

www.fnmoc.navy.mil/PUBLIC/
US Navy Fleet Numerical Meteorology and Oceanography Center site. Europe COAMPS (Coupled Ocean/Atmosphere Mesoscale Prediction System) model output with 10nm grid

www.nlmoc.navy.mil/home1.html
Charts and text forecasts for the whole Mediterranean from another
US Navy site
NATO sea areas used in text warnings are the same as those used in Turkish bulletins (*see above*)

http://ows.public.sembach.af.mil/index.cfm
US 21st Operational Weather Squadron weather site

www.arl.noaa.gov/ready/cmet.html
US Air Resources Laboratory website.

www.weathercharts.org
An enormous number of links to Internet weather chart sources

www.eurometeo.com
Charts and text forecasts for the whole Mediterranean, both free and by subscription

www.weatheronline.co.uk
Charts and text forecasts for the whole Mediterranean, both free and by subscription

www.theyr.net
A subscription service providing both Hi-Res charts and GRIB files

http://weather.unisys.com/gfsx/index_eur.html
Unisys weather charts for Europe

www.wetterzentrale.de
A collection of weather charts from different sources. Of particular interest:
www.wetterzentrale.de/pics/sfanim.html   and
www.wetterzentrale.de/pics/Rsfloc.gif
are charts of lightning and thunderstorm activity; also
www.wetterzentrale.de/topkarten/fsfaxsem.html
Fax charts with an archive of past data

http://meteocentre.com/lightning/eur_sfuk_anim.gif
http://meteocentre.com/lightning/map_sfuk.php?time=0&lang=fr&map=Europe
Another real time chart for lightning and thunderstorm activity

www.euclid.org/realtime.html
Alternative real time chart for lightning activity

www.franksingleton.clara.net
A very interesting site about weather information aboard boats, by a former Met
Office senior forecaster

www.westwind.ch
A collection of charts from different sources, grouped by type of model

www2.wetter3.de/fax.html
A nice collection of different fax chart sources (UK, Germany, US, etc), both surface
and upper level

www.windguru.cz
Forecasts for selected locations with a subscription service for more detailed data

www.buoyweather.com
Forecasts for selected locations with a subscription service for more detailed data

www.meteoconsult.com
A private company offering both free content and subscription services, together with
GRIB files

www.saildocs.com
A service which allows receiving text based internet information by email. Besides
providing GRIB files, it also allows receiving the textual content (no images) of user-
defined web pages by email, or text weather forecasts

www.navimeteo.eu
A company offering (among other services) the possibility of discussing weather
outlook and routing options by phone, directly with a forecaster

www.metmarine.com
Text weather forecasts sent to UK registered cell phones. Available areas as of now are
coastal areas of Spain, France, Turkey and Ionian Greece

www.mailasail.com
A company specialised in on-board communications, providing also email weather
information service

www.meteoalarm.eu
Although not exactly for mariners, a site indicating Alert situations (wind, drought,
flooding, etc) all over Europe, with contributions from National Met Offices

Sites with High Resolution Charts

(pressure, wind fields, wave heights, etc)

Besides several National Met offices or private sites mentioned above, high resolutions charts can also be found at the following internet addresses.

www.meteoblue.ch
Hi-res charts for the whole Mediterranean

www.capemalta.net/maria/pages/atmosforecast.html
Hi-res charts for the whole Mediterranean from ETA model

www.politicheagricole.it/UCEA/dalam/index.htm
Hi-res charts for the Mediterranean west of the Aegean Sea

www.ilmeteo.it/marine.htm
Hi-res charts for various areas, see headings 'Venti e Mari' and 'Mappe Meteo'

www.infomet.fcr.es
Hi-res charts for Europe, from Barcelona University

www.arpa.emr.it/sim/?mappe_numeriche/numeriche&vento_10_metri
Hi-res wind and pressure charts for Adriatic. *See under 'Mare' section.*

www.meteosimtruewind.com
Hi-res charts for Western Mediterranean

www.meteoliguria.it/level1/model.html
Hi-res charts (21 and 6·5km spacing) for the Central and Western Mediterranean

www.sar.sardegna.it/servizi/meteo/previsioni.asp
Hi-res charts for Sardinia and Western Central Mediterranean

www.lamma.rete.toscana.it/wrf-web/index.html
www.lamma.rete.toscana.it/ww3/ww3_viewer.html
Hi-res charts for the whole Mediterranean, some areas available in more detail

www.poseidon.ncmr.gr
Hi-res charts for the Aegean from the ETA Model

www.noa.gr/indexen.html
The National Observatory of Athens site, Hi-res charts for the Aegean Sea; forecasts for selected points of the whole Mediterranean from the same source also available at www.eurometeo.gr/

http://forecast.uoa.gr/forecastnew.html
Hi-res charts for the whole Mediterranean and Greece

www.adriamet.info/adriamet/previsioni.html
Hi-res charts for the Adriatic, and thunderstorm/precipitation radar images for the Northern half

GRIB FILES

A relatively recent and user-friendly way of retrieving weather information is by means of GRIB files (from Gridded Binary, a standard code for meteorological data dissemination).

These are coded numeric files of very limited size, which can easily be received as email messages; automatic decoding software then displays all the information on an electronic map or nautical chart.

Apart from areas with cell phone connectivity or internet cafés, limited size email can be exchanged in the open sea through free services like Airmail (for licensed radio amateurs, see www.winlink.org for more information) or commercial ones like Sailmail (www.sailmail.com/); an SSB transceiver and a Pactor modem are the usual required equipment.

Available data relevant for cruisers is usually wind (strength and direction), pressure, sea state, etc.

GRIB files can usually be downloaded for different intervals and forecasting horizons. Every file contains weather data related to a series of evenly spaced geographical points distributed on a grid.

Here is an example of what a GRIB chart may look like.

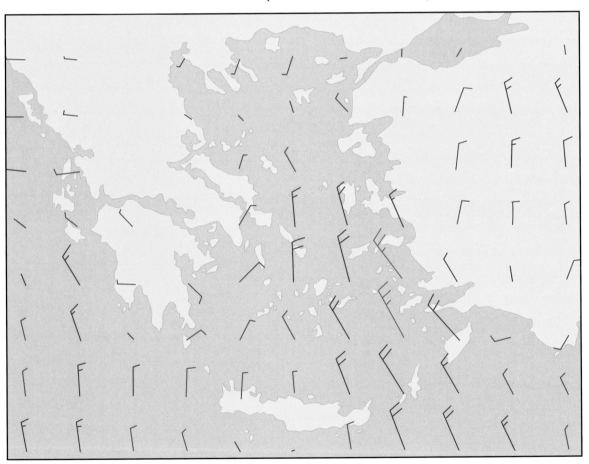

An example of what a GRIB chart may look like

A few words of caution: while having a set of arrows indicating wind speed and direction at several moments in the future may be considered the ideal outcome for sailors, one should keep in mind the following.

a. Many GRIB data is taken from synoptic/global type models (*see the description of different model characteristics above*), as it has been indicated, one should always check the type of native model used in preparing GRIB files, and be particularly attentive to their different characteristics before relying on them for Mediterranean weather forecasting;

b. Many GRIB files are 'raw', i.e. they are crude model figures which have not gone through the human screening of an experienced weather forecaster, who instead intervenes for example before the final output of common weather charts; anomalies or discrepancies are not unusual, either inside a given model output, or inside a series of following model 'runs';

c. GRIB data is computed for a grid of geographical points with a given spacing: if two points are spaced 60M for example, there is a high level of uncertainty in interpolating figures for a third point halfway between them, especially in areas where local features may have a great impact on the weather like it is often the case in the Mediterranean. One should always check and refer to the grid spacing of the original model.

Beside those mentioned above, a few providers of input data and/or decoding software and GRIB viewers are listed below.

www.grib.us/
A very user-friendly free GRIB viewer

www.globalmarinenet.net/grib.htm

www.navcenter.com/

www.raymarine.com/raymarine/

www.progrib.com/

www.xaxero.com/

www.maxsea.com/

http://mscan.com/

Another free GRIB viewer can also be downloaded at the Winlink/Airmail site mentioned above

www.winlink.org

Meteo France offers a subscription service called Navimail, where among other things GRIB files from high resolution Aladin model are available for the Western Mediterranean. More details on:

www.meteofrance.com/FR/services/navimail/installation_en.jsp

COASTAL TEXT BULLETINS EXAMPLES

Spain

The Instituto Nacional de Meteorología issues three weather bulletins for sea areas up to 20M from the coast.

The morning bulletin is issued on day D at around 1000 local time and is valid until 2400 of day D; a first evening bulletin is issued on day D at around 2200 local time and is valid until 2400 of day D+1; a third evening bulletin is issued at around 2200 local time of day D and is valid until 2400 of day D+2.

It is divided into four parts:

1. Avisos: Warnings, strong wind warnings, if any
2. Situación general y evolution: A short description of pressure features
3. Predicción: Forecasts
4. Informe de estaciones: Local station reports

Example of a Spanish bulletin

DIA XX A LAS 20 UTC.

1. AVISO A LAS 18 UTC DEL DIA XX:
   NO HAY AVISO

2. SITUACION A LAS 12 UTC DEL DIA XX Y EVOLUCION: ANTICICLON DE 1032 AL OESTE DE AZORES, CON CUNA DE 1016 HASTA EL SUROESTE DE FRANCIA, ESTACIONARIO Y DEBILITANDOSE UN POCO. DEPRESION DE 1002 EN EL NORTE DE ITALIA, ESTACIONARIA Y RELLENANDOSE HASTA 1008. BAJAS PRESIONES DE ENTRE 1002 Y 1006 EN EL INTERIOR DE AFRICA.

3. PREDICCION VALIDA HASTA LAS 24 UTC DEL DIA XX+1:
   AGUAS COSTERAS DE MALAGA: COMPONENTE OESTE FUERZA 3 A 5 ROLANDO Y AMAINANDO POSTERIORMENTE A VARIABLE FUERZA 2 A 3 Y A COMPONENTE ESTE AL FINAL DEL DIA. MAREJADILLA CON AREAS DE MAREJADA AL PRINCIPIO.
   [...]

4. INFORME DE ESTACIONES LAS 18 UTC DEL DIA XX:

   PROVINCIA DE MALAGA:
   - ESTEPONA: SIN DATOS
   - FUENGIROLA: OESTE FUERZA 3 CON RACHAS DE 5
   - MALAGA: ESTE FUERZA 3 CON RACHAS DE 5
   [...]

Example of Bulletin with the Outlook for the following two days

PREDICCION METEOROLOGICA PARA LAS ZONAS COSTERAS DE CATALUNA DESDE LAS 00 UTC DEL DIA XX+1 HASTA LAS 24 UTC DEL PROXIMO DIA XX+2.
DIA XX A LAS 1000 UTC

1. PARA EL DIA XX+1 A LAS 00 UTC SE ESPERA: CUNA ANTICICLONICA SOBRE EL NORTE PENINSULAR CON PRESIONES DE 1016 SOBRE LA COSTA CATALANA.

2.- PREDICCION VALIDA DESDE LAS 00 HASTA LAS 24 UTC DEL DIA XX+1. AGUAS COSTERAS DE GIRONA: EXTREMO NORTE: NW FUERZA 5 AMAINANDO Y ROLANDO POR LA TARDE A SW 3–4. MAREJADA DISMINUYENDO A MAREJADILLA POR LA TARDE.
   RESTO: NE 3 ROLANDO A SUR 2–3 POR LA TARDE. MAREJADILLA.
   [...]

3. PREDICCION VALIDA DESDE LAS 00 HASTA LAS 24 UTC DEL DIA XX+2. SW FUERZA 3–4.

France

Meteo France regular bulletins are updated three times a day, at 0700, 1200, 1900 Local Time.
They are divided into seven parts:

1. Gale warnings
2. Situation (a short description of the main pressure features)
3. Forecast for the following 24 hour period, divided into:
   TEMPS (cloudiness), VISIBILITE (visibility), VENT (wind), MER (sea state), HOULE (swell)
4. Forecast for the following 12/24hour
5. Outlook for the following 24 hour period
6. Local station reports: Wind direction and strength - Sea state – Pressure - Visibility
7. Other significant phenomena, if any

Example of a bulletin issued around 1300 Local Time

DE PORT CAMARGUE A SAINT-RAPHAEL
Elaboré le jour D à 11H30.
1   Avis de grand frais à fort coup de vent, numéro XXX, pour toutes les zones.
      FIN DE VALIDITE : jour D+1 à 08h UTC.
2   SITUATION GENERALE LE JOUR D A 06H00 UTC ET EVOLUTION.
      Dépression 1003 hPa sur la plaine du Pô. Dépression 1010 hPa se creusant l'après-midi vers Nice se
      déplaçant ensuite vers l'Est la nuit. Anticyclone 1032 hPa sur les Açores quasi stationnaire.
3   Après-midi du jour D et nuit suivante.
      TEMPS : devenant moins nuageux.
      VISIBILITE : bonne.
      VENT:- à l'Ouest du Cap Croisette, vent de secteur Ouest force 5 à 6, tournant Nord-Ouest
      en début de nuit.
      - à l'Est du Cap Croisette, vent de secteur Sud-Ouest force 6 à 7 avec rafales, ponctuellement force 8
      vers les Iles d'Hyères jusqu'au soir.
      MER: agitée, forte vers le large.
      HOULE: confondue avec la mer du vent.
4   Jour D+1.
      TEMPS : Beau.
      VISIBILITE : bonne
      VENT:- à l'Ouest de Cassis, vent Nord-Ouest force 5 à 6, revenant temporairement Ouest l'après-midi.
      En soirée vent de Nord-Ouest 4 à 5.
      - à l'Est de Cassis, vent de secteur Ouest force 6 à 7 avec rafales, mollissant force 5 à 6 la nuit.
      MER: agitée, forte vers le large.
      HOULE: confondue avec mer du vent.
5   Evolution pour le jour D+2.
      Vent de secteur Ouest force 4 à 6, mollissant en fin de nuit. Beau temps. Mer peu agitée à agitée.
6   A 11 Heure Locale on observait:
      Vent – Mer – Pression - Visibilité
      Noeuds - hPa - M
      CEPET: WNW 24 - peu agitee – 1011 - >15
      LE LEVANT: W 24 - 1010
      CAMARAT: NW 16 – agitee - >15
7   Phénomènes importants du jour D+3.
      néant.

The strong wind warning is called BMS, Bulletin Météo Spécial.
BMS-Côte (Coastal wind warning) are issued when the wind is forecast at 7 Bft (Grand Frais) or above.
BMS-Large (Offshore wind warning) are issued when the wind is forecast at 8 Bft (Coup de vent) or above.

Italy

Italian bulletin is called 'Meteomar'. It is broadcast continuously on Channel 68, both in English and Italian.

Forecasts cover the whole Mediterranean and depending on propagation may often be heard at great distance from the coast, from a longitude west of Sardinia to the south of Sicily, and as far as the Ionian Greek islands.

Technically, it is an offshore bulletin as it is related to wide sea areas, but the same text is also used for coastal forecasts. When sailing in areas where coastal features have a relevant impact on wind characteristics, it is advisable to keep in mind that the bulletin may not consider many of these local modifications, hence adjust accordingly the forecast contents.

Meteomar sea areas are different from the GMDSS grid, *see chart above, under Radiotelephony paragraph.*

The bulletin is updated four times a day: at 0000, 0600, 1200 and 1800.

Forecasts made at 0000 and 0600 are valid until 1800 of the same day, while the Outlook is valid for the oncoming 12 hours.

Forecasts made at 1200 and 1800 are valid until 0600 of the following day, while the Outlook is valid for the oncoming 12 hours.

The final part of the bulletin is a forecast for wind and sea state for four intervals of 12 hours each.

It is divided into four parts

1. Warnings: gale and thunderstorm warnings
2. Weather situation: a short description of the main pressure features over the whole Mediterranean.
3. Forecasts up to (1800 or 0600, *see above*) and following 12 hour outlook.
4. Wind and sea state during four 12 hour intervals following the end of the period given in number 3.

Example of a bulletin issued at 1800 UTC

It may be worth having a look at its structure as it takes a bit to get used to the 'mechanical voice', which can be confusing as words are read individually, one at a time. The final line for example would sound like: 'Southern – Adriatic – sea – west – four – sea – three – northwest – four – sea – three – south – three – sea – three – east – three – sea – four'.

1. WARNINGS:
   Thunderstorms under course: Northern Adriatic Sea
   Thunderstorms forecast: Nil.
   Gales under course: Northwesterly 7 on Corsican Sea and Sardinian Sea;
   Southwesterly 7 on Ligurian sea and Southern Tyrrhenian east side.
   Gales forecast: Northwesterly 7 on Corsican sea and Sardinian Sea.

2. WEATHER SITUATION:
   A low of 1000hPa on Northern Adriatic Sea. Weak cold front on North-Central Italian
   Seas is rapidly moving eastward. Seasonal low on Levantine basin.

3. FORECAST up to 0600 UTC of tomorrow, and 12-hour outlook
   Ligurian Sea: Southwesterly 6 weakening - Partly cloudy weakening – Good visibility – Rough sea weakening
   Outlook: southwesterly 6 – Partly cloudy
   [...]
   Alboran Sea: Southwesterly 4 – Partly cloudy – Good visibility – Slight sea – Outlook: Southwesterly 4 – Fair.
   [...]

4 WIND AND SEA STATE over Italian seas from 0000 UTC of the day after tomorrow at 1200 hour intervals.
   Corsican Sea: West 5 Sea 5 / West 5 Sea 5 / West 4 Sea 5 / West 4 Sea 4
   [...]
   Southern Adriatic Sea: West 4 Sea 3 / Northwest 4 Sea 3 / South 3 Sea 3 / East 3 Sea 4
   [...]
   End Meteomar

6067

Croatia

Bulletins are divided into four parts

1. Warnings: Strong wind and thunderstorm warnings.

2. Synopsis: a short description of pressure features.

3. Forecast for the following 12 hours.

4. Outlook for the ensuing 12 hours.

Example of Croatian bulletin

1. Warning
   Isolated thundery rain showers, mainly in the Central Adriatic late in the day and during the night. Gusts of SW and NW wind 30–40 knots, diminishing tomorrow.

2. Synopsis
   A trough with frontal disturbance has approached the Adriatic from the northwest.

3. Weather forecast for the Adriatic for the first 12 hours.
   In the North Adriatic SW and W wind 12–26 knots. In the rest of the Adriatic mainly SW, in the Central Adriatic SW and NW gradually increasing to 12–26 knots. Sea 3–4. Visibility 10–20km. Variably cloudy with scattered rain, isolated rain showers and thunder, mainly in the central Adriatic late in the day and during the night.

4. Weather forecast for the next 12 hours
   Mostly clear, but with variable cloudiness in places and with a risk of isolated rain showers and thunder, mainly in the central Adriatic around the middle of the night and in the north Adriatic around midday. Moderate to strong W and NW wind gradually diminishing to light. Sea slight and moderate, gradually calming to smooth and slight. Air temperatures will drop.

Greece

Bulletins are divided into four parts.
1. Warnings: Strong wind and thunderstorm warnings.
2. Synopsis: a short description of pressure features.
3. Forecasts valid 24 hours.
4. Outlook for the following 12 hours.

Example of a Greek bulletin

NATIONAL METEOROLOGICAL SERVICE
ATHENS MARINE METEOROLOGICAL CENTRE
WEATHER AND SEA BULLETIN FOR SHIPPING
DATE AND TIME OF ISSUE … … UTC

1. NO GALE

2. SYNOPSIS OF SURFACE WEATHER CHART DAY 'D' AT XXXX UTC
     RELATIVELY HIGH PRESSURES 1014 OVER CENTRAL MEDITERRANEAN SEA AND
     1008 OVER EAST TURKEY. LOW 1000 OVER BULGARIA AND 1003 EAST OF RHODES

3. FORECAST FOR 24 HOURS
    NORTH ADRIATIC
    WEST NORTHWEST 4 SOON LOCALLY 5. MODERATE LOCALLY POOR. THUNDERSTORM

    CENTRAL ADRIATIC
    WEST NORTHWEST 4 VERY SOON 5 SOON LOCALLY 6. MODERATE TEMPORARILY POOR.
    THUNDERSTORM VERY SOON
    […]
    SOUTH IONIO
    WEST NORTHWEST 4 LATER LOCALLY 5. MODERATE

    PATRAIKOS
    WEST 3 LOCALLY 4. MODERATE

    KORINTHIAKOS
    WEST NORTHWEST 5 SOON LOCALLY 6. GOOD
    […]
    KASTELLORIZO SEA
    WEST NORTHWEST 4. MODERATE

    RODOS SEA
    NORTHWEST 3 LOCALLY 4. GOOD

    KARPATHIO
    NORTHWEST 4 LOCALLY 5. GOOD

    WEST KRITIKO
    WEST 4 LOCALLY 5. GOOD

    EAST KRITIKO
    WEST NORTHWEST 4 LOCALLY 5. GOOD

    SOUTHWEST AEGEAN
    WEST 4 LOCALLY 5 SOON 5 SOUTH OF 36.30 LOCALLY 6. GOOD
    […]

4. OUTLOOK FOR 12 HOURS
    STRONG NORTHWEST WINDS OVER HELLENIC SEAS

Turkey

Bulletins are divided into three parts.

1. Warnings

2. Situation (a brief description of weather features)

3. 24 hour forecasts, divided into four periods of six hours each

Example of a bulletin issued at 1500 UTC, valid from 1800 UTC of day D to 1800 UTC of day D+1

1. Near gale warning over Aegean and Jason.

2. At 1200GMT there is 1004hPa low pressure center over Cyprus.
   No significant change in this system during the period.

3. Forecast for 24 hours from XX1800 UTC up to XX1800 UTC

CRUSADE	1800–0000	0000–0600	0600–1200	1200–1800
GALE	No Gale	No Gale	No Gale	No Gale
WEATHER	Partly Cloudy	Partly Cloudy	Partly Cloudy	Partly Cloudy
WIND	W & SW 3–5	W & SW 3–5	W & SW 3–5	W & SW 3–5
SEA	1·0 to 2·0m	1·0 to 2·0m	1·0 to 2·0m	1·0 to 2·0m
VISIBILITY	Good	Good	Good	Good

AEGEAN	1800–0000	0000–0600	0600–1200	1200–1800
GALE	Near Gale Warning	Near Gale Warning	No Gale	No Gale
WEATHER	Few Cloudy,	Few Cloudy,	Few Cloudy,	Few Cloudy,
	N & NE 4–6,	N & NE 4–6,	N & NE 4–6,	N & NE 4–6,
WIND	NW 5–7 in S	NW 5–7 in S	NW 4–6 in S	NW 4–6 in S
SEA	2·0–3·0m,	2·0–3·0m,	2·0 to 3·0m	2·0 to 3·0m
	2·5–3·5m in S	2·5–3·5m in S		
VISIBILITY	Good	Good	Good	Good

APPENDIX II

Wind roses

The following Figures report monthly wind roses for the whole Mediterranean.

They graphically show the average wind conditions for a one degree area (latitude by longitude) around their position on the map.

Every rose shows a set of arrows from eight directions (N, NE, E, SE, S, SW, W, NW), whose length is proportional to the frequency of wind blowing from that direction. If the frequency is above 30%, a number is indicated in place of a very long arrow.

The number of barbs at the end of the arrow indicates the average Beaufort force. The frequency of calms is indicated by the number inside the circle.

While wind roses can be interesting, cruisers are strongly advised not to overvalue their informative content.

A few cautionary remarks may be helpful in interpreting them.

1. As it has been shown in the book, Mediterranean wind patterns are often very different from those that can be experienced in the open ocean or in tropical areas, where regularities in speed and direction are much more common.

   There are no features like 'Trade winds' or 'Westerlies' which might help with passage planning, except perhaps the few seasonal regularities we have indicated about some sea areas. During the course of a given month, winds may blow from several different directions, and with greatly varying speeds.

   As an aside, US sailors will be delighted to know that there is no sea ice in the Mediterranean (except occasionally in some quiet canals of the Venice lagoon, during the coldest of winters), and that tropical storms and hurricanes do not occur: winds may (rarely) reach hurricane force, but never with the duration and extension of tropical meteorological phenomena.

2. Wind roses depict average speeds, not prevalent speeds. They do not indicate how much wind speed can vary around the reported average.

   As an example, a wind rose showing a prevalent northerly wind direction of say Force 5, might well represent the average of northerly winds blowing half of the time at force 2–3, and half of the time at Force 7–8, which of course is quite a different thing for sailors who by looking at the wind rose might wrongly expect a nice passage in a 20 knot wind.

   To add to variability, 'half of the time' might well mean twelve hours a day, two days out of four, or one week out of two, which of course have very different meanings in terms of navigation and passage planning.

3. Whenever no prevalent direction is shown (wind rose arrows of roughly the same length), again one should remember that the wind rose represents a monthly average. As an extreme example, a wind rose showing an equal 25% frequency of winds form the N, S, E and W might well represent

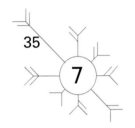

Wind rose

The length of each arrow is proportional to the frequency of the wind. The number of barbs indicates Beaufort force. The number in the centre indicates percentage of calms.

For example, in the wind rose above NW winds show a frequency of 35% with an average 4 Bft, winds from the N, W and SE have a similar frequency, and respectively 3Bft, 4Bft and 3Bft strengths. During the month, there is a 7% frequency of calm wind.

winds blowing for one week from the N, the following week from the W, and so on, which again is a different matter altogether from the sailor point of view.

A wind rose with no prevalent wind direction might as well be originated by observations taken from an area frequently crossed by depressions with varying paths all over it. Again, with a bit of careful on-the-spot planning sailors can try and maximise their chances of favourable wind conditions.

It cannot be overstressed that flexibility in adapting passage planning to the actual and forecast weather situations is by far the best way of maximising the chances of favourable wind conditions, and enjoy at their best the countless wonderful experiences that Mediterranean cruising can offer.

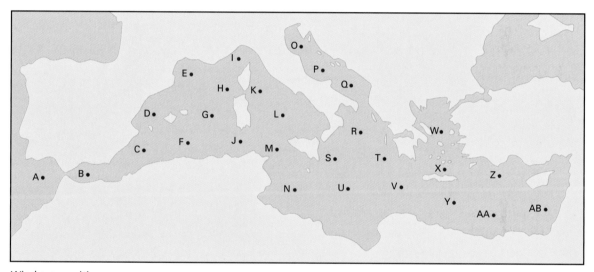

Wind rose positions

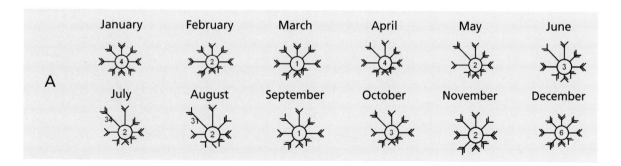

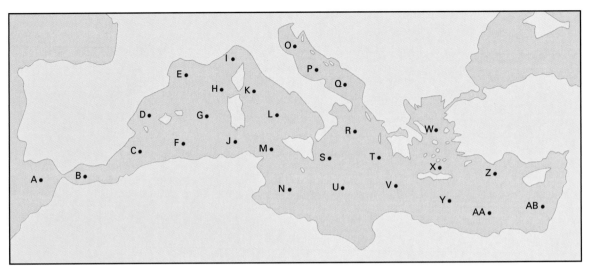

Wind rose positions

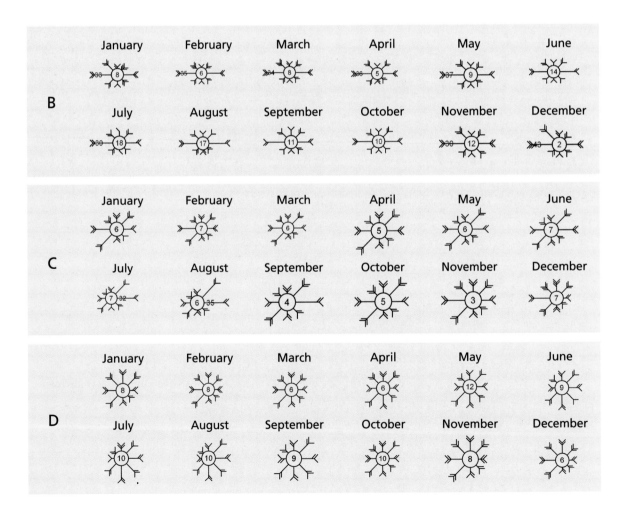

E

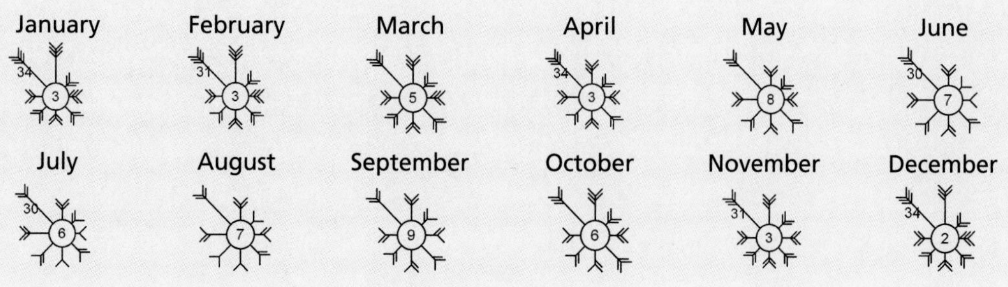
January
34
3
February
31
3
March
5
April
34
3
May
8
June
30
7
July
30
6
August
7
September
9
October
6
November
31
3
December
34
2

F

January
4
February
4
March
3
April
5
May
11
June
13
July
10
August
8
September
5
October
8
November
2
December
4

G

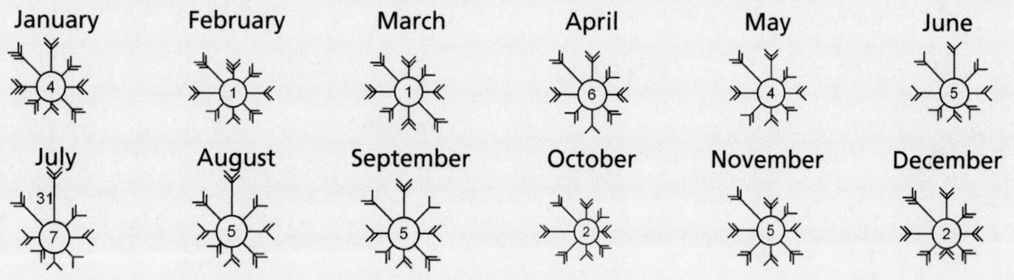
January
4
February
1
March
1
April
6
May
4
June
5
July
31
7
August
5
September
5
October
2
November
5
December
2

H

January
2
February
5
March
2
April
9
May
7
June
8
July
31
7
August
8
September
9
October
10
November
6
December
6

I

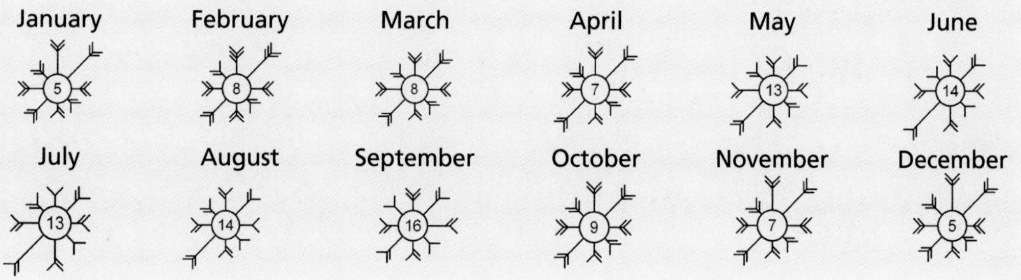
January
5
February
8
March
8
April
7
May
13
June
14
July
13
August
14
September
16
October
9
November
7
December
5

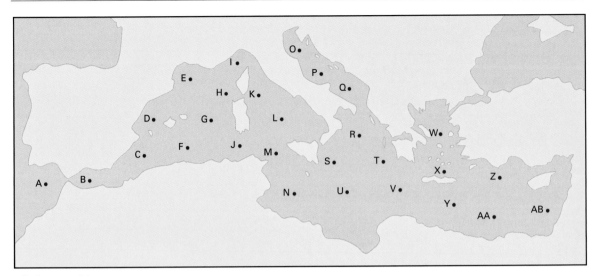

Wind rose positions

J

	January	February	March	April	May	June
	3	4	5	6	7	8
	July	August	September	October	November	December
	8	7	7	6	5	4

K

	January	February	March	April	May	June
	6	4	3	5	6	6
	July	August	September	October	November	December
	10	6	7	7	4	3

L

	January	February	March	April	May	June
	6	6	4	5	12	11
	July	August	September	October	November	December
	12	14	13	8	5	4

M

	January	February	March	April	May	June
M	2	3	3	3	5	7
	July	August	September	October	November	December
	6	5	5	4	3	2

	January	February	March	April	May	June
N	0	0	3	0	8	0
	July	August	September	October	November	December
	4	13	8	0	0	0

	January	February	March	April	May	June
O	3	7	16	16	22	16
	July	August	September	October	November	December
	26	13	13	4	6	6

	January	February	March	April	May	June
P	9	3	6	10	10	5
	July	August	September	October	November	December
	9	5	20	18	0	2

	January	February	March	April	May	June
Q	7	4	1	7	4	10
	July	August	September	October	November	December
	13	7	5	6	1	2

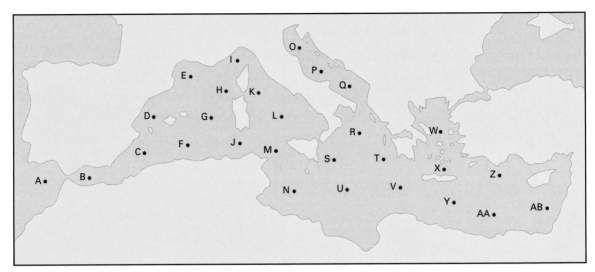

Wind rose positions

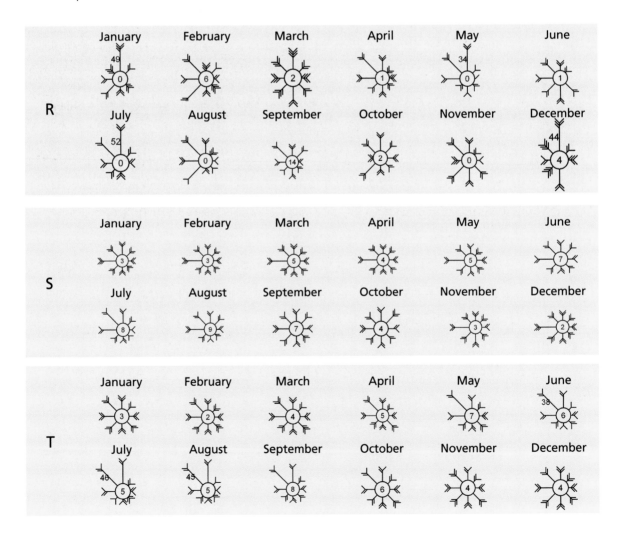

U

January	February	March	April	May	June
2	4	4	3	4	7
July	August	September	October	November	December
6	31 / 32 / 6	6	4	3	3

V

January	February	March	April	May	June
2	1	2	3	4	4
July	August	September	October	November	December
2	31 / 1	5	5	3	2

W

January	February	March	April	May	June
3	3	32 / 4	7	7	31 / 8
July	August	September	October	November	December
50 / 4	46 / 3	39 / 5	38 / 4	3	2

X

January	February	March	April	May	June
4	4	6	34 / 8	34 / 9	34 / 31 / 4
July	August	September	October	November	December
42 / 42 / 0	44 / 39 / 2	42 / 1	5	2	34 / 1

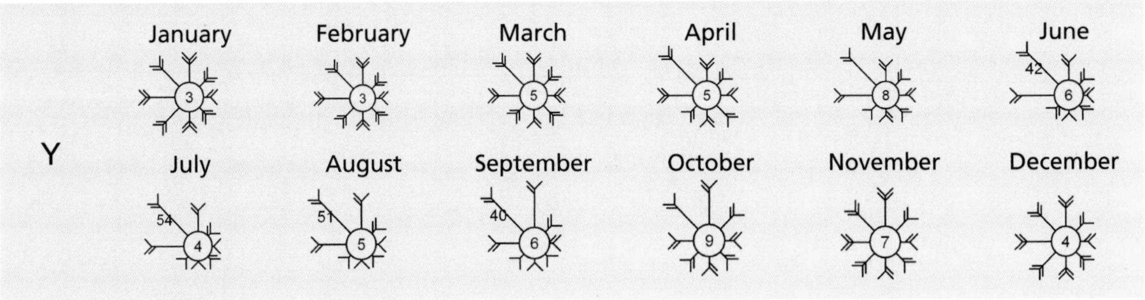
Y
January
February
March
April
May
June
July
August
September
October
November
December

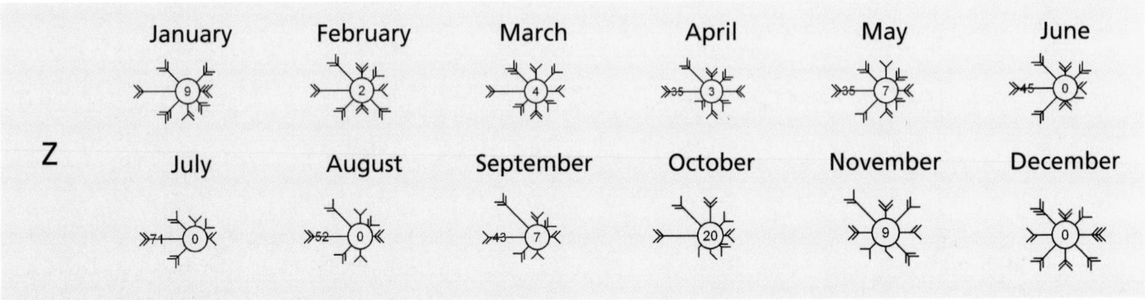
Z
January
February
March
April
May
June
July
August
September
October
November
December

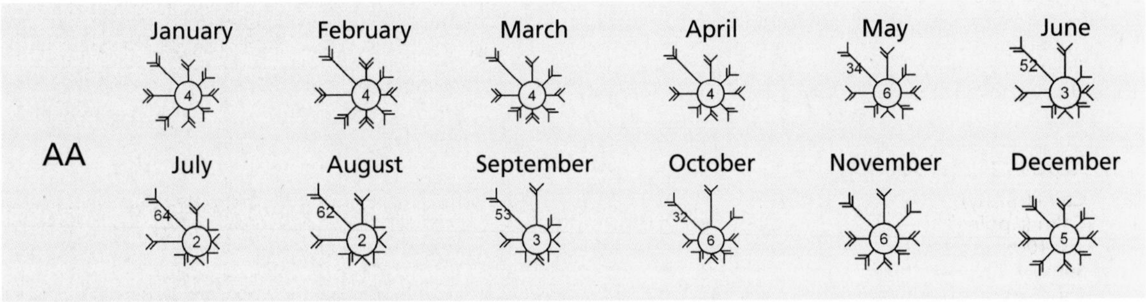
AA
January
February
March
April
May
June
July
August
September
October
November
December

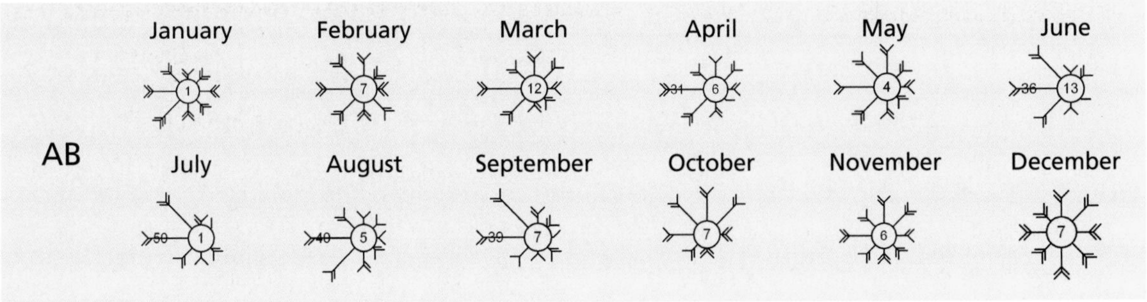
AB
January
February
March
April
May
June
July
August
September
October
November
December

APPENDIX III
Dictionary of useful meteorological terms

English	French	Spanish	Italian
Beaufort scale (wind speed)			
0 Calm	Calme	Calma	Calma
1 Light air (1–3kn)	Très légère brise	Ventolina	Bava di vento
2 Light breeze (4–6kn)	Légère brise	Flojito	Brezza leggera
3 Gentle breeze (7–10kn)	Petite brise	Flojo	Brezza tesa
4 Moderate breeze (11–15kn)	Jolie brise	Bonancible/Moderado	Vento moderato
5 Fresh breeze (16–21kn)	Bonne brise	Fresquito/Brisa fresca	Vento teso
6 Strong breeze (22–27kn)	Vent frais	Fresco/Brisa fuerte	Vento fresco
7 Near gale/Moderate gale (28–33kn)	Grand frais	Frescachón/Viento fuerte	Vento forte
8 Gale (34–40kn)	Coup de vent	Temporal	Burrasca
9 Strong gale (41–47kn)	Fort coup de vent	Temporal fuerte	Burrasca forte
10 Storm (48–55kn)	Tempête	Temporal duro	Tempesta
11 Violent storm (56–63kn)	Violente tempête	Temporal muy duro	Tempesta violenta
12 Hurricane (>64kn)	Ouragan	Temporal huracanado	Uragano
Sea state scale (wave height)			
0 Calm (glassy)	Calme	Calma	Calmo
1 Calm (rippled) (<0·10m)	Calme (ridée)	Rizada	Quasi calmo
2 Smooth (0·10–0·50m)	Belle	Marejadilla	Poco mosso
3 Slight (0·5–1·25m)	Peu agitée	Marejada	Mosso
4 Moderate (1·25–2·50m)	Agitée	Fuerte marejada	Molto mosso
5 Rough (2·50–4·00m)	Forte	Gruesa	Agitato
6 Very rough (4–6m)	Très forte	Muy gruesa	Molto agitato
7 High (6–9m)	Grosse	Arbolada	Grosso
8 Very high (9–14m)	Très grosse	Montañosa	Molto grosso
9 Phenomenal (>14m)	Enorme	Enorme	Tempestoso
Visibility (nautical miles)			
Good (>5nm)	Bonne	Buena	Buona
Moderate (2–5nm)	Médiocre	Moderada	Discreta
Poor (0·5–2nm)	Mauvaise	Escasa (neblina, calima)	Scarsa
Fog (<0·5nm)	Brume	Niebla	Nebbia
Useful terms used in bulletins			
Afternoon	Après-midi	Tarde	Pomeriggio
Become (of wind)	S'orienter, devenir	Orientarse	Orientarsi
Build (of a high)	S'établir, Se renforcer	Reforzar	Rafforzarsi
Clouds, cloudy	Nuages, nuageux	Nubes, nuboso	Nuvole, nuvoloso
Decrease	Diminuer, mollir	Amainar, Disminuir	Diminuire, calare
Deepen (of a low)	Se creuser	Profundizarse	Approfondirsi, Intensificarsi
Drifting	En déplacement	Desplazamiento	Spostamento
East	Est	Este	Est

English	French	Spanish	Italian
Evening	Soir	Noche	Sera
Expected	Attendu, Prévu	Previsto/Esperado	Atteso, Previsto
Fall (pressure)	Baisse	Baja	Calo, diminuzione
Fine weather	Beau temps	Tiempo bueno, soleado	Bel tempo
Fill (of a low)	Se combler	Rellenarse	Colmarsi
Flat low	Marais barométrique	Pantano barometrico	Pressione livellata
Flow	Flux	Flujo	Flusso
Fog	Brouillard/Brume	Niebla	Nebbia
Forecast	Prévision	Prediccion	Previsione
Frequent	Fréquent	Frecuente	Frequente
Front, cold	Front froid	Frente frío	Fronte freddo
Front, occluded	Front occlus	Frente ocluído	Fronte occluso
Front, warm	Front chaud	Frente caliente	Fronte caldo
Gradient	Gradient	Gradiente	Gradiente
Gust	Rafale	Rafaga, Racha	Raffica
Hail	Grêle	Granizada	Grandine
Heat low	Dépression thermique	Baja termica	Depressione termica
High	Haute pression, Anticyclone	Alta, Anticiclon	Alta pressione/ Anticiclone
Improve	Améliorer	Mejorar	Migliorare
Imminent	Imminent	Inminente	Imminente
Increase	Augmenter	Arreciar, Aumentar	Aumentare, Rinforzare
Initially	Initialement	Al principio	Inizialmente
Intensify	S'intensifier	Intensificarse, Aumentar	Intensificarsi
Isolated	Isolé	Aislado	Isolato
Less	Moins	Menos	Meno
Lightning	Eclair	Relampago	Lampi, fulmini
Local	Locale	Local	Locale
Low	Basse pression/ Dépression	Baja, Depresión	Bassa pressione/ Depressione
Lull	Accalmie	Calma	Calma
Moderate	Modéré	Moderado	Moderato
More	Plus	Más	Più
Morning	Matin	Mañana	Mattino
Move (weather system)	Se déplacer	Desplazarse	Spostarsi
Night	Nuit	Noche	Notte
No changes	Sans changements	Sin cambios	Senza cambiamenti
North	Nord	Norte	Nord
Occasional	Occasionnel	Ocasional	Occasionale
Overcast	Couvert	Cubierto	Coperto
Outlook	Tendance ultérieure	Tendencia posterior	Tendenza (ulteriore)
Prevailing	Dominant	Dominante	Dominante
Quickly	Rapidement	Rapidamente	Rapidamente
Rain	Pluie	Lluvia	Pioggia
Ridge	Dorsale/Crête	Dorsal, Cuna	Dorsale, Promontorio
Rising (pressure)	En augmentation	En aumento	In aumento
Shallow low	Dépression relative	Baja relativa	Depressione relativa
Shift (of wind direction)	Tourner, S'orienter	Rolar	Orientarsi, Virare
Shower	Averse	Chubasco, chaparrón, Aguacero	Rovescio
Slowly	Lentement	Lentamente	Lentamente
South	Sud	Sur	Sud
Squall	Grain	Turbonada	Groppo
Stable	Stable	Estable	Stabile
Stationary	Stationnaire	Estacionario	Stazionario
Strong	Fort	Fuerte	Forte
Swell	Houle	Mar de fondo	Mare lungo
Thunderstorm	Orage	Tormenta	Temporale
Trough	Thalweg/Creux	Vaguada	Saccatura
Variable	Variable	Variable	Variabile
Visibility	Visibilité	Visibilidad	Visibilità
Weak	Faible	Débil	Debole
Weaken	S'affaiblir, s'affaisser	Debilitarse	Indebolirsi
West	Ouest	Oeste	Ovest

INDEX